REFUGEE WORKFORCE

"Chris' book and the stories he tells are timely. It needs to be read and repeated. The economic case he makes is very compelling. But it's the stories he tells of refugees; the hardships they face before and after their arrival to the United States; and how the employers who took chances with them were rewarded with an awesome committed workforce that truly make you hopeful in today's political climate."

—Prayag Narula, CEO, Lead Genius

"Industrial manufacturing is facing labor shortages in both skilled and unskilled positions across the US. The approach described by Chris and Katie promote an effective use of refugees to bridge the labor gap in a thoughtful, structured and legal way to create sustained economic growth. This book is a must read for manufacturing companies desperately seeking motivated and dependable employees."

—Doug Gates, Global Chair of Industrial Manufacturing, KPMG

"With firsthand experience in placing refugees in businesses, Chris and Katie dispel the myths about refugees and establish the vital role refugees play in the U.S. workforce and economy. Since the passage of the Refugee Act in 1980, Refugee workers have been an invaluable contributor to the American economy."

—Ali Noorani, Executive Director, National Immigration Forum

"I'm so glad the team at Amplio put their knowledge about workforce development into this book! I've been working on the frontlines with refugees, helping them rebuild their lives, for over a decade and I don't know anyone better in the U.S. to speak about our refugee friends' unique ability to fill labor shortages and support economic growth."

—Jeremy Courtney, President, Preemptive Love Coalition

"This message has the ability to change every workplace and every team. Putting action to this book makes all our lives better."

—Jeff Sh   People

D1716053

"...a really good resource for employers who are new to employing those who have been through the refugee experience. From my years of working in refugee resettlement, this publication can be very helpful to those employer placement specialists at agencies who need tools to open up new employer relationships. Thanks for doing the work to market this capable workforce. Our whole U.S. field will appreciate this."

—Jane Leu, Founder & Former CEO, Upwardly Global

"The book highlights the impact of refugees as an investment in the future of America and an example of the American dream."

—Heval Kelli, Heart surgeon at Emory Clinical Cardiovascular
Research Institute, former Syrian Refugee,
Founder of Young Physians Initiative

"I've seen firsthand how refugees are underrated and overlooked as strong positive contributors to communities & local economies. This book serves as a practical resource for companies looking to hire and retain dependable team members — improving their own competitiveness while helping both refugee and host communities thrive together."

—Premal Shah, Senior Advisor & Co-founder, Kiva.Org

"Chris and Katie have written a wise and compelling book. I've lived in the refugee-majority community of Clarkston for over seven years, and experienced firsthand the facts stated clearly and honestly here. And I've seen with my own eyes the flourishing Amplio Recruiting promotes, both in the lives of refugees here in Georgia and in the businesses that believe in the refugee workforce and back that belief up in their hiring practices. As Chris says, refugees are not victims who need our sympathy, nor are they terrorists who warrant our fear. No message could be more timely at this juncture in our country's history."

—Kitti Murray, President, Refuge Coffee

"The 'war for talent' is one of the greatest competitive challenges facing any leader, company or industry today. Employers need workers who are motivated and energized to learn, grow and develop within evolving workplaces. Refugees, by and large, are naturally motivated to create stable homes for their families after enduring often unthinkable circumstances and endlessly transitional years. Chris and Katie practically communicate the reasoning and processes for hiring refugees in a compelling way throughout this book. Having now trained and employed refugees for more than a decade, I'm happy this resource exists to support any business owner facing labor and talent challenges as they head towards a stronger future for their business."

—Tara Russell, Senior Vice President,
Global Impact at Carnival Corporation

"As an artist, authentic art is a direct reflection of us. As an immigrant, that reflection looks like hope, perseverance, and opportunity. That's what Amplio has given to other folks like myself. Now that they've put pen to paper and created a tangible way for the world to read, I can't wait for everyone else to know just how special these folks are."

—Ron Bultongez, American Idol Finalist, Recording Artist

"For over forty years those who have fled wars and catastrophic famine such as those in Vietnam and Somalia have been given the chance for new life in the United States. In this timely and important work, Refugee Workforce details how these incredible survivors have continuously defied the odds in not only escaping the crisis that claimed so many lives, but by actually improving the communities and economy in the places where they have been resettled. Now more than ever, policy makers, business leaders, and everyday people need to understand the incredible contribution refugees have made to the United States. We are safer and more prosperous because of them."

—Jason Clarke, Co-Founder & President, Seek the Peace (SEEK)

REFUGEE WORKFORCE

The Economic Case for
Hiring the Displaced

Chris Chancey & Katie Gibson
of Amplio Recruiting

AMPLIO
RECRUITING

CONTENTS

INTRODUCTION

Meet Orlando Morrow, hard-working production supervisor at a global food distribution company, where he's worked since 1998. The company veteran is no stranger to the challenges of leadership, but lately, he can't seem to find or retain the number of employees he needs to keep pace.

Their job is simple: cut down large blocks of cheese into smaller portions, and package for distribution. *But workers aren't staying.* No matter how many initiatives he's tried, or extra hours he's put in, a lack of dependable employees is keeping his department from being profitable and productive.

He's tried traditional staffing companies, who send seven, eight, nine apathetic new-hires each week, but nearly every single one of them inevitably quits. A mere ten workers are left to do the work of thirty, racking up loads of overtime— even on the weekends.

Orlando knows that continued strain will lead to even more loss, but he feels powerless to fix the situation.

Where can Orlando find dependable employees who will show up on time and do the work, and stay?

. . . .

Meet Mohammad Soda, an orderly and soft-spoken 18-year-old refugee from Syria. His family was among the first forced to flee from their nation's infamous Civil War that has since displaced more than 12 million people.[1]

Mohammad has been working to support his family since he was barely a preteen. But here, in America, he is disheartened by the seeming lack of opportunity. He wants nothing more than to work hard and support his family, and pursue his dream of becoming a doctor one day.

Unfortunately, the experience he's gained during his time as a refugee doesn't translate well to a resume. As a new arrival with developing English skills and few connections, he fears he will end up like many others before him— working a dead-end job at the local chicken factory.

Where can Mohammad find a job that will allow him the opportunity to prove himself, and rebuild the life he lost when he was forced to flee his home country?

. . . .

Heated immigration debates rise to a boil as an unprecedented 70.8 million, and counting, are displaced worldwide.[2] While politicians fight to limit immigration, the U.S. economy struggles under the weight of a growing problem: a gaping hole in skilled trades workers.

As of May 2019, job openings soared to over 7.5 million, leaving business owners desperate for skilled and dependable labor.[3] With unemployment rates at their lowest in over half a century, where can these companies turn for the help they need?[4]

The labor shortage problem is growing, but we believe the answer to it has also been growing in cities across the United States: the refugee workforce.

THE LABOR SHORTAGE IS GROWING, BUT WE BELIEVE THE ANSWER TO IT HAS ALSO BEEN GROWING IN CITIES ACROSS THE UNITED STATES: THE REFUGEE WORKFORCE.

Refugees are individuals who have been forced to leave their home country because of war, persecution, or natural disaster. Resettled in countries across the world, they must quickly acclimate to their new environments.

They are resilient, and they are motivated—factors leading many refugees to take humble jobs well below their occupational and educational capacity in order to provide for themselves.

In 2014, I began to recognize how these two needs, when put together, could serve as a solution to each other. Now, after five years of staffing American companies with the refugee workforce, I am more convinced than ever that hiring refugees is not only a socially responsible decision, but also a *profitable* decision. And that's what I hope to prove to you through this book! I couldn't be more excited about pulling back the curtain on what I believe is the best-kept secret for the health of America's economy.

In part one, we'll look deeply into the realities of both the current U.S. job market, and the plight of the refugee. I'll lay out the case for why, at the most basic level, hiring refugees is a viable solution to the three most common needs of American companies: workers who are legal, dependable, and drug-free.

In part two, I'll reveal the proven cycle that, when set into motion, can get businesses out of the rut of constant hiring, micromanaging, and rehiring. We'll look at how the refugee workforce is helping businesses across the country break free from this exhausting cycle, and gain traction like never before. After that we'll explore the concept of "growth mindset" (versus fixed mindset), and explain why the majority of refugees have it. Then I'll show you how growth mindset employees, plus the added bonus of diversity, can grow future leadership and boost innovation and creativity.

Hiring the refugee workforce is a win-win solution for both American companies and resettled refugees. After exploring the *abundant* benefits of hiring refugees to businesses, we'll look at the opposite side of the coin. As it turns out, employment is a lot more than just a means to make money. A good job provides security, and promotes acclimation and healing.

In our final chapter I'll address the need to build "bridges" to better engage the refugee workforce. There are so many businesses, organizations, and governments making great strides in this area we can learn from. We'll look at different policies and models promoting health for refugees, companies, and the overall economy.

Here's what you **won't** find in this book:

- A magic formula for instant success. Every good relationship requires work. Companies looking to integrate refugees into their team will more than likely need to make changes to business as usual. But I do promise to walk you through common hurdles you might encounter, and help you see why the end result is worth the effort.

- A pity party for refugees. In fact, you'll get quite the opposite. Refugees don't want to be looked at as victims, but as valuable contributors. We'll take an honest look at their challenges, but we'll celebrate their fierce tenacity to overcome them.

Here's what you **will** gain from reading this book:

- A viable plan for not only addressing your immediate labor shortage needs, but promoting long-term growth within your company.

- Honest observations based on five years of experience of placing refugees in companies across the U.S.

- A nonpartisan approach that is for businesses, for people, and for the overall economy.

- An understanding of the refugee resettlement journey, and some ways we can help these individuals integrate into the American workforce, and utilize the fullest extent of their talents and experiences.

If you were here, I'd order some falafel and hummus from my friend Malek's catering business. We'd sit down in a corner of our teeming Amplio office over delicious Syrian food, and I'd tell you about how I found myself in the staffing business. I'd tell you about some amazing companies, and the innovative world-changers who run them. I'd share equally heartbreaking and inspiring stories of our refugee employees, like Amnobe, Rafiq, and Werga. We'd talk business, economy, policies, and dream about making our little corners of the world a better place.

Since I can't be with you in person, I'm grateful this book can do that. The following pages are filled with those stories, statistics, and experiences I would share with you. And I hope, when you're finished, you will send me an e-mail (chris@ампliorecruiting.com) and share your feedback.

So go order your favorite ethnic food and pull up a seat. Let me tell you how I stumbled upon America's most underrated workforce.

ONE | ROOM AT THE TABLE

"We are handcuffed."

Truth be told, I never set out to be in the staffing business. Nor have I always felt a burden for the refugee community. But life's experiences have a way of shaping our passions and experiences into *purpose*, don't they?

The only thing I knew was that I liked helping people. And I realized, along the way, that business, when leveraged intentionally, could be used to do so. That simple awareness, plus a chain of extraordinary events only God could have set into motion, led me to where I am today.

I don't consider myself a hero, but I do work with a lot of them. Individuals who have overcome excruciating loss and made the decision to not only pick themselves up and carry on, but to make the world a better place for others in the process.

This book is about them— the refugee workforce. Their stories. Their triumphs. Their grit. And their undeniable value to our world, and in the American workplace.

But before we dive into their stories, I feel it makes the most sense to start with *my* story. Because, after all, *how does a middle class white guy from South Georgia find himself running a refugee staffing agency?*

The answer really isn't all that impressive. I'm just an ordinary guy who found himself at the intersection of two great needs, and I was just crazy enough to think I could be a part of the solution. Mine isn't a rags-to-riches or even a pain-to-purpose story. It's a story of showing up and saying "yes" to life, and working hard.

What I didn't know when I started was that my "yes" would open opportunities for me I could have never imagined: helping restore lives and businesses, speaking in front of crowds of business leaders, owning the world's first B Corp Certified staffing company, and writing the book you're holding in your hands.

My story starts in my hometown of Waycross, Georgia, where I was born and raised. My family taught me to honor God by working hard, playing hard, and caring for those in need. After high school, I followed my dreams a few hours north to Athens, where I attended the University of Georgia. There, I earned a degree in journalism and—most importantly— met and married my incredible wife, Sarah.

Together, we chased another dream several states west to Denver, Colorado, where I began studies at Denver Theological Seminary. I thought I wanted to be a pastor, mostly because I wanted to help people. Turns out, God had other plans for me.

During this time, my wife and I had the privilege of managing a Chick-fil-A restaurant location with $2.6 million in annual sales. As a full-time student and more-than-full-time general manager, those days were hectic. But it was a pivotal season in my life, because it changed the way I understood the power of leveraging business to impact the world.

After completing my Master's degree in Christian studies and business stewardship, Sarah and I were eager to move back to Georgia to be close to family. We bought a house near Atlanta, in the city of Decatur, unknowingly planting ourselves on the fringes of a wonderfully unique community (we'll get to that shortly).

My wife busied herself growing her thriving wedding planning business, and I took on a job at HOPE International, a leading global microfinance organization. I loved how my job, raising funds to help entrepreneurs in the developing world start and grow businesses, gave me the opportunity to utilize my passions and talents. The position allowed me to sit down regularly with highly successful American businessmen and businesswomen who were investors in HOPE's network.

As an aspiring entrepreneur, I reveled in the opportunity to glean wisdom from these individuals. The year was 2012, and the economy was beginning to heal from the disastrous "housing bubble" which sparked one of the worst recessions in our nation's history. However, despite steadily rising market demand, the individuals I spoke to expressed frustration that their companies weren't growing at the rates they had predicted.

The problem, they told me, was maintaining their workforce. "We just can't find good employees," they would say. The problem piqued my curiosity. *Wasn't it just yesterday that unemployment was high, and Americans were begging for work?*

The more I sat down with marketplace leaders, the more I tuned in to the challenges they were facing. Labor shortages were restraining what would, otherwise, be a season of immense growth.

It wasn't long before I realized the enormity of the situation— growing labor shortages were not only a threat to the health of companies, but would eventually thwart the growth of our entire American economy.

. . . .

GROWING LABOR SHORTAGES WERE NOT ONLY A THREAT TO THE HEALTH OF COMPANIES, BUT WOULD EVENTUALLY THWART THE GROWTH OF OUR ENTIRE AMERICAN ECONOMY.

Fast-forward seven years, to today.

My premonitions about labor shortages were right— but the situation has grown far worse than I could have ever anticipated.

At the time of this book's writing there are 7.5 million open jobs, and only 5.8 million individuals hypothetically "looking" to fill them.[5*]

For those in search of work, the job market is a buffet of opportunity, but for those doing the hiring, *it's slim pickings.*

The article first alerting me to the severity of the situation revealed that in California and several other states, millions of dollars' worth of fruits and vegetables were dying in the field for lack of workers to harvest them.[6] It was shocking to me, and I couldn't get the problem out of my mind. Years later, farmers across the nation are *still* desperate to attract and maintain enough workers to keep food on our tables, much less their own.

Farming isn't the only industry shortages have impacted. If you're keeping pace with the news, you've probably noticed that no state has been left untouched...

In the Research Triangle Area of North Carolina, the lack of skilled tradesmen has driven house prices sky-high. Shortages are so severe that many contractors have taken to "poaching" workers off of competing companies' job sites.[7]

---

[*] Please note: These numbers fluctuate month to month, and though the gap seems to be steadily widening at this point, we'll use these two numbers as placeholders throughout the book.

In Houston, Texas, a crisis-level lack of truck drivers is strangling the growth of its burgeoning oil fields. Trucks are needed at every stage of the production and distribution process. And with new regulations and a retiring generation of truckers, it's likely the current 50,000 driver deficit will get worse before driverless technology can take the wheel.[8]

Across the nation, manufacturing is back on the rise. President Donald J. Trump's initiatives to bring manufacturing back to the U.S. seem to be going as planned, except for one glaring problem: companies are now struggling to meet demand. Despite desperate attempts to attract new workers, even unskilled positions sit unfilled for months at a time. One company, in In Manitowoc, Wisconsin, shared that they had turned away business "to the tune of more than $10 million," simply because they "can't hire enough people…"[9]

The reality is that these are just a *handful* of recent cases I've come across. Companies across the nation are feeling the pinch. However, the reality of the situation really hits home when I talk to local businesses.

Every day I get messages from business owners lamenting the same problem, best summarized in an email I received just this morning: **"We are operating only a small team, but are handcuffed by a labor shortage to execute our projects."**

Handcuffed by labor shortages. While labor shortages certainly fall under the category of being a "good problem," as indicative of a thriving economy, they are a problem nonetheless. It's only a matter of time before our demand for goods exceeds the ability to meet that demand, and our economic growth folds.

So what happened to our nation's dependable workforce?

While the most popular blanket answer to that question seems to be "Baby Boomers retiring from the workforce," further studies reveal not one, but *several* socioeconomic changes over the past decade that have led to our disappearing workforce.

An entire book could be written about how we got here, but I'll leave that to the experts. For now, I'll briefly describe the main causes, so we can better discern our potential solutions.

Baby Boomers

To start, *yes*, the Baby Boomers' exit from the workplace is a significant contributor to our nation's labor shortage problem. An estimated 10,000 individuals are retiring from the workforce every day.[10] While opening positions for the next generation is generally a positive event, this time around there is one big glaring caveat: *the next generation isn't filling them.*

While Baby Boomers gravitated toward skilled trades and lifetime careers, Generations X, Y and Z prefer more flexible and dynamic work. This growing divergence is becoming most noticeable within the manufacturing, construction, and healthcare (i.e. nurses, home health aides, medical assistants, etc.) industries, where thousands of positions are already unfilled. Despite a strong push for up-and-coming generations to pursue trades, few are catching the vision they can make a decent paycheck without the expense of a college education.

Undocumented Immigrants

A second demographic shift our nation has seen in the past decade is the quiet exodus of undocumented immigrants from the workforce. Between 2007 and 2016, the U.S. workforce grew by 10 million workers, but at the same time *lost* an estimated 400,000 unauthorized immigrants.[11] Construction, service, and farming industries have endured the brunt of this "hit." (Remember the article that first caught my attention about fruit dying on the vine in California?)

> A CLOSER LOOK REVEALS THE MAJORITY OF THESE NEWCOMERS HAVE SIMPLY FILLED THE JOBS AMERICANS AREN'T WILLING TO TAKE.

While I wholeheartedly believe regulations and due process are good and necessary, we cannot deny the fact that our country's measures to eradicate unauthorized immigration have caused significant hardship on entire industries. The complaint for years has been immigrants are taking jobs from Americans, but a closer look reveals the majority of these newcomers have simply filled the jobs Americans aren't willing to take.

We'll look more into this subject in a later chapter, but for now we must acknowledge that, while attempting to fix one problem, we have created an entirely different one altogether.

Prime-age Men
A third demographic shift, and most baffling to me, is the steady decline of prime-age men (ages 25-54) engaged in the workplace. "Over the past 50 years, the percentage of prime-age men who are 'inactive'— neither working nor looking for work— has more than tripled... Economists generally expect men between the ages of 25 and 54— those who are in the prime of their working lives— to have the highest rates of employment. But... seven million prime-age men— 11.5 percent of the population— are staying away from the labor market."[12]

While some attribute the rise of women in the workplace for this phenomenon (as more men are choosing to stay home and raise families), statistics tell a different, albeit vague, story. Many are blaming "job polarization," due to a lack of middle-skill work, for the trend.[13] However, it is important to note that **a staggering 47 percent of inactive prime-age males cited disability as their reason for not participating in the labor force,** making it, *by far,* the largest share of any of the reasons given for inactivity.[14]

While I cannot say for certain, I believe there is a strong link between the high level of disability claims and our next, and final, problem we'll cover.

Substance Abuse
The final major contributor to our nation's disappearing workforce, that we'll discuss here, is the rising prevalence of substance abuse.

With over half of American companies administering drug tests as part of their job interview process, failures have climbed to the highest rate since 2004[15] In states where recreational marijuana has been legalized, many companies have been forced to relax their stance on employee usage in order to maintain their workforce, but for some this simply isn't an option. In "safety sensitive" industries such as transportation, construction and manufacturing, elevated surfaces and heavy machinery require sober and alert employees, as one single misstep could have *deadly* consequences.

There is evidence that our current opioid crisis may be a leading cause behind the disappearance of prime-age men from the workplace. Injured workers (usually male) often turn to opioids to relieve their pain and get back on the worksite ASAP. However, there are two problems to this "solution." First, consumption of these powerful painkillers has been shown to *extend* recovery time, lengthening the victim's time spent out of work and on disability.[16] Second, opioids are *highly* addictive. **Studies show an incredible 8-12 percent of individuals who are prescribed opioids become caught in a vicious cycle of addiction, and remain out of work indefinitely.[17]**

My oversimplified explanations here represent only the most prevalent causes behind our disappearing workforce, but I hope you're beginning to see the big picture.

We can create new jobs all day long, but we're just spinning our wheels with no workers to fill them.

> COMPANIES ARE NOT ONLY STRUGGLING TO ATTRACT NEW WORKERS— THEY'RE FIGHTING TO KEEP THE ONES THEY HAVE.

The reality is that companies are not only struggling to attract *new* workers— they're fighting to keep the ones they have.

As the unemployment rate has dropped, employees quitting their jobs has soared. I talk to businessmen and businesswomen every day who express their frustration at fighting a constant battle for employees who will simply show up on time and do their job.

The only way to get businesses unstuck and moving forward is to help them identify viable solutions that will not only fill vacant positions, but also reduce costly turnover.

So what are our options?

Recently, a lot of attention has been focused on the need to "re-skill" Americans. Companies across the nation have reacted out of desperation to implement on-the-job training programs and incentives to attract potential talent. While this is certainly a noteworthy initiative, Americans just aren't responding at the rates anticipated.

Perhaps the problem isn't re-skilling Americans after all.
It's re-motivating them.

With 7.5 million jobs available to the 5.8 million individuals currently looking, it is obvious there is room for anyone who is willing to work. In our country, we are blessed with *so much* opportunity. Men and women of all races and cultures have greater access to higher education and the job market, than ever before. But with all this *increased* opportunity, it seems the desire to work has *decreased* among Americans. The number of should-be contributors dropping out of the workforce has increased. So where does this leave companies? Must we stand by and wait for our nation's disappearing workforce to reappear? Or is there an alternative solution we can turn to?

Do dependable employees who are not only legal to work, but capable of learning new skills, and largely devoid of substance abuse still exist anymore? If so, *where?*

. . . .

After moving back to Atlanta, my wife and I enjoyed exploring our vibrant community. As we ventured out for errands and meals, one thing became clear: many of our new neighbors were not from around here. We encountered painted signs hanging above the doors of businesses written in unfamiliar languages, delicious new foods originating from a variety of countries, women in hijabs, and men in brightly colored Dashikis.

We soon learned the local community of Clarkston and surrounding areas was "home" to more than 37,000 refugees who have been resettled here since the 1990's.[18] Clarkston's affordable housing and proximity to Atlanta made it an ideal landing pad for the displaced. Once a predominantly white community, Clarkston is now commonly referred to as the "most diverse square mile in America," with over half of its population hailing from countries around the world.[19]

My wife can attest to the fact that I quickly became the "annoying white guy" who constantly attempted to strike up conversations with neighbors. I was intrigued because many of my coworkers at HOPE International were in countries these refugees were fleeing from. I had peers in The Democratic Republic of the Congo and Burundi, and I had even spent time with our staff in Haiti. My genuine curiosity drove me to ask them questions about where they were from, how they came here, and what they missed most about their home countries.

Much to my surprise, these individuals didn't just humor me— they took the time to engage in conversation. I learned many of my new neighbors had once held dignified positions. They were doctors, engineers, teachers, government officials, and business owners. Some had even helped *our* military with day to day operations.

Then, they shared with me their journey of leaving all of it behind. *It was absolutely heartbreaking.* More heartbreaking than anything, though, was the desperation in their voices when they asked not for pity, or even a handout—but simply for a good job.

Overwhelmed by the aggressive American job market, and lacking connections, the majority of these talented, educated, and experienced individuals were working jobs well below their capacity— if they even had a job at all.

They would plead, "Can you help me find a good job? No one is hiring."

Again, I was intrigued. I knew this was far from the truth. There were plenty of Atlanta companies in need of dependable employees. But this was *their* reality.

> **THEY HAD BEEN SELLING, CONSTRUCTING, SEWING, AND PROGRAMMING BACK IN THEIR HOME COUNTRIES BEFORE THEIR LIVES WERE UPROOTED.**

The refugee community was a labor pool no one seemed to be tapping into. *But why?* It wasn't that refugees didn't want to work. On the contrary, many of them possessed the strongest desire I had ever encountered. They had been selling, constructing, sewing, and programming back in their home countries before their lives were uprooted.

They were eager to rejoin the marketplace. *They just needed an invitation.*

. . . .

This was how I found myself at a pivotal crossroads, positioned between two problems I innately understood could be the solution to one other.

It seemed to me that no one else was seeing what I was seeing: Companies needed legal, motivated employees to fill crucial shortages, and the refugee community was an incredibly viable source.

I mulled over the idea of starting a business that could connect these two groups together. Refugees simply needed someone to acknowledge their skills, strengths, and job experience and give them a boost into the workplace. Companies needed someone to introduce them to this overlooked, but highly motivated labor pool that could help them attain the growth they were seeking. I loved my job at HOPE, but felt drawn to be a part of the solution to the problem set before me.

About the time I was considering this new venture, I heard a quote from Pastor Leonce Crump who said, "May your table be filled with people who are not like you." The power of these words struck me so profoundly. I was convinced to take the leap.

In 2014 I founded Amplio Recruiting with zero experience in staffing— just a compelling belief in the potential social and economic impact of connecting the two needs. The name "Amplio" came from the Spanish word for "ample." I chose it specifically to communicate our beliefs about the job market: there are an ample number of good jobs to go around, and an ample number of dependable individuals to fill them.

I quickly realized my greatest challenge to success would not be convincing companies they needed dependable workers— they already knew that. The challenge would be convincing them that a group of people who had been so grossly misdefined by the media would be the best fit for their open positions.

Refugees are most often portrayed in one of two ways: a charity case, or a terrorist threat— neither of which hold true.

Portrayed as a *charity case*, they are reduced to nothing more than a group of people who have experienced horrific tragedy, so they should live out their days on American public assistance. Even though they have overcome many insurmountable challenges, they now need endless handouts, and their experience, here in America, should be socialism.

I could not agree less.

Have they faced more than their fair share of challenges? Certainly. But the majority of refugees I've met are not looking for handouts, and "charity case" should not define them. However, the alternative portrayal isn't much better—

Portrayed as a *terrorist threat*, refugees are distorted as a group of people who we should watch closely. Their differing religions and cultural beliefs are a threat to our values and way of life so we should restrict their access to fully participate in our society. We should control their environment, make government-level decisions concerning their well-being, and their experience, here in America, should be communism.

This portrayal is equally disturbing. Yes, refugees speak, dress, and act differently but they are certainly not terrorists — rather victims *of* terrorists (we'll get to that more, shortly). And, from my experience, they are not looking to force their beliefs and customs on anyone. The suspicion that they came here with an agenda to undermine our safety and freedom melts away once you sit down face to face with any of these new Americans.

I recognized this truth early on: the refugees in my community didn't fit into either of these two political boxes, driven by either pity or blind fear. Instead, there was a third box that nearly all refugees did fit into: **contributors.**

They didn't want endless handouts. They wanted opportunity. They wanted to add value to their communities. They wanted to pay taxes, and participate in the educational system. The idea of capitalism was enticing, and they wanted their shot at the American dream— just like the generations of immigrants that had come to the U.S. before them.

Not a charity case. Not a terrorist threat. *A workforce.*

And, from what I could tell, the best-kept secret to revitalize American companies.

With this conviction, I set out to show businesses the value of, what I coined, the "refugee workforce." If putting those two words together makes you uncomfortable, or seems like an oxymoron, then I'm glad you picked up this book, so I can guide you down the path I've been on for the past five years.

One by one, I began matching refugees to open positions. To be honest, it wasn't nearly as easy as I thought it would be. There were so many questions to be answered, methods to be explored, and hurdles to overcome. I made many mistakes, and even shut the business down at one point.

But a God-ordained pivot, a lot of perseverance, and an amazing workforce, laid a solid foundation for the company to emerge.[*] It wasn't long before Amplio employees were adding value in dozens of companies across Atlanta— from manufacturing headlights for Tesla, to cutting fiber-optic cable for Google.

Around this time, Luke Keller became my business partner and contributed to a huge boost in sales. Sana Hajizada, a refugee from Afghanistan, joined shortly after to manage payroll so we could keep up with the growth. The positive feedback began rolling in. Companies that had tried other staffing solutions to no avail were coming to us, confirming my expectations: *the refugee workforce was working.*

A microelectronics developer saw improved efficiency.

A food distributor experienced a drastic reduction in turnover.

The athletic club noted greater all-around work ethic, as their new refugee employees were inspiring *everyone* to bring their "A" game.

---

[*] For a video interview about the experience, visit **www.refugeeworkforce.com.**

Owners, managers, and co-workers— even those who were skeptical from the start—were now singing the praises of their newest team members. But companies weren't the only ones benefiting from the partnership. Refugees and their families were, too.

Mohammad, Birhane, and Kisembo learned English.

Claudy was able to afford essential medications for his mom's heart condition.

Sana and Amnobe were able to buy homes for their growing families.

Stories from companies and refugees alike kept pouring in—*both were thriving.*

. . . .

The "If Gap"

The most common pushback we get, when people hear about our work, is the old argument, "Refugees are taking jobs from Americans." So before we go any further, let's look at a "perfect world" scenario to see if this viewpoint is valid.

There are 7.5 million jobs sitting open in the U.S. at the moment I'm writing this sentence.[20] We've seen how retiring baby boomers, substance abuse, and the high inactivity of prime-age men in the labor force are contributing to this huge deficit.

There are 5.8 million individuals listed as "unemployed" right now. These are able-bodied 16-65 year olds who are actively looking for a job, but for whatever reason have not been hired.[21]

If every one of these unemployed Americans took an open job tomorrow, we'd still have a 1.7 million worker gap to fill if we want to keep our economy growing.

Let's take it one step further, for a moment, and imagine the best-case scenario.

First, you need to know the U.S. Bureau of Labor and Statistics tracks every detail of who is and is not participating in the labor force and for what reasons. They divide the labor force into three categories: employed, unemployed and individuals not participating in the labor force at all.

Remember, those that are unemployed have actively sought a job in the last month but have yet to find one. Those not participating in the workforce have made no effort to get a job in the past month. Mostly this includes full-time students, full-time moms or those that are retired.[22]

One alarming side note to reiterate here is that in September of 1954, the month my dad was born, the percentage of prime-aged men not active in the workforce sat at 2%. As I'm writing this book, the BLS reports over 11% of prime-aged men are now inactive in the workforce.[23] If the past 65 years are any indication of the next 65, we must become more innovative in our approach to sustain economic growth.

Now back to our best-case scenario. There is a subset of those identified as not participating in the labor force referred to as discouraged workers. Discouraged workers report they are not currently looking for work for one of the following reasons:

- They believe no job is available to them in their line of work or area.

- They have previously been unable to find work.

- They lack the necessary schooling, training, skills, or experience.

- They face some type of discrimination.[24]

As I'm writing this book the BLS reports the number of discouraged workers stands at 425,000.[25] That's a lot of people saying they would take a job if it were offered to them, but have become completely beaten down by the process of getting a job and the rejection that comes along with it. So let's take all the unemployed individuals and all these discouraged workers across the country not participating in the workforce and match them up with open jobs.

Even with this idyllic employment utopia projected on our current labor shortage, we still fall way short— our best estimates would put us at approximately 6.2 million individuals added to the job market.

That is IF every unemployed person obtained a job and IF those that have given up even looking for a job became gainfully employed.

> **THE BEST-CASE SCENARIO WOULD STILL LEAVE US WITH APPROXIMATELY 1.3 MILLION VACANCIES NEEDING TO BE FILLED TO KEEP THE ECONOMY CHURNING.**

This best-case scenario would still leave us with approximately 1.3 million vacancies needing to be filled to keep the economy churning.[*]

(To see a stunning visual depiction of the "If gap," visit the resource page of our book website at www.refugeeworkforce.com. I highly recommend sharing this video and data set on your socials as a way to engage in an educated discussion on issues of immigration.)

Room at the Table
As you can see, *there is ample room for everyone at the table.*

---

[*] Math breakdown:
7.5M job openings
5.7M unemployed + 425K discouraged = 6.2M
7.5M - 6.2 M = 1.3M gap!

No matter which political party you identify with, and all moral arguments aside, there is a strong case for the tremendous economic impact of refugees and immigrants in the workplace. After five years in my role, I am more resolute than ever that the refugee workforce is the best-kept secret for revitalizing U.S. companies, and sustaining the overall economy.

My goal in writing this book is not to debate politics, or pretend to be an economic expert. Neither is it to throw shade on the American work ethic.

My goal is simply to share my experience, and communicate the value of the largely overlooked refugee workforce. In the following pages, I'll explain why helping these individuals integrate into the workforce is not only ethical— it's economical.

First, I'll dispel some common myths by taking a close look at the realities of refugee resettlement. We'll learn more about our new neighbors, and hear their stories firsthand.

Then, I'll lay out for you why, at the most basic level, refugees "check the boxes" when it comes to three of the most prevalent workplace needs. We'll hear from some great companies who have led the way in hiring them. Their stories will reveal how, beyond just filling positions, refugees make *exemplary* employees. We will explore these distinct attributes, and learn how nurturing them helps employers attain even higher levels of productivity and innovation.

Finally, we'll look at the restorative nature of work, and its benefits to the refugee. And we will dream of what our society would look like if we pursued better pathways to integrate these motivated individuals into the workforce.

Maybe you're reading this book because you're already deeply engaged in supporting the refugee community. Maybe you've been asking yourself, *is there a better way?*

If that's you, I want to say thank you for moving beyond apathy and stepping in to take part in this important conversation. As you read the following pages, I pray the ideas found within would challenge you to consider the best way to empower refugees to restore their lives, regain dignity, and to *thrive*.

Maybe you're a businessman or businesswoman and you've spent this chapter nodding in agreement. You feel like the labor pool has gone dry, and you're all out of options. You've heard about companies who have integrated refugees into their workforce, but you're doubtful it could ever work for you. You've picked up this book to see if there is enough compelling evidence to give it a shot. *I'm so excited for you.*

I believe the stories and statistics herein will give you the confidence to press forward, and as you do, you will experience the growth you've been looking for.

There's also the chance you're reading this book because you're skeptical about refugees, and whether they belong in the American workplace. That's okay, too. I'm glad you're searching out answers, and hope the words in these pages will help you come to a positive conclusion about the refugee workforce.

I'm glad you're on this journey with me. I believe we're at a pivotal place in our country's history. The decisions we make now will impact our social and economic health for years to come. My greatest hope is that the truths found here will make their way into the hands of policy makers and influencers who will not just half-heartedly agree with them, but initiate positive change accordingly.

As you read this book, I encourage you to ask yourself the question: how can I be a part of the solution? And when the answer comes to you, I hope you will simply say "yes" like I did.

Without any further delay, allow me to introduce you to the refugee workforce.

TWO | FEAR & FAKE NEWS

"If you don't sweat, you don't eat."

BOOM.

Zinah's eyes open. She sits up in bed.

Bombs are not unusual in Baghdad, but this one sounded close. *Too close.* She takes a deep breath to calm her pounding heart, then climbs out of bed to begin preparing for the day.

Life in Iraq has always been turbulent, as far back as Zinah can remember.

The Iran War.
Kuwait.
Desert Storm.

But the start of this latest war had given her hope that it might *finally* be the last; believing American troops could secure peace for Iraq.

That would not be the case. Instead, it led to the rise of ISIS, and sectarian violence claiming the life of Zinah's older brother, "the twin of her soul."

Her mother, a professor at a prestigious university, and her father, a former

pilot for Saddam Hussein, were forced to flee because of their positions of influence. Their sudden departure left 24-year old Zinah with the responsibility to care for her younger siblings, while going to school to earn her degree in biology.

They sleep behind multi-locked doors. Every morning she checks underneath her car for bombs before starting the engine, then checks again at red lights *just in case.*

Tragedy and anxiety replay in her head, over and over again.

The loss of her parents.
The loss of her brother.
The bombs.
The death threats.

Suddenly, she is approached. They put a gun to her head and ask her to identify as either Sunni or Shia.

Zinah knows that the wrong answer will mean a quick end for her. She takes a deep breath and responds…

Zinah's answer satisfies her attackers.

Tears blur her vision as they lower their guns and allow her to drive away. She would not become another number on her nation's growing death toll that day.

Though she would never forget the experience, she decided right then and there that tragedy and anxiety would not define her life—*she would.*

She made the decision to apply for refugee status, with the hope that her and her siblings could find a new home—any place safer than Baghdad.

. . . .

Fear Mongering and Fake News

The refugee crisis is one of the greatest tragedies of our time. Currently, there are more than 25.9 million refugees, adding to a total of 70.8[26] million displaced individuals worldwide— numbers that rise daily. Every minute an estimated 31 people are forcibly displaced from their homes due to war, violence, persecution, and natural disasters.[27]

The statistics are staggering. Still, many continue to turn their backs on, or worse— *attack*— this vulnerable people group.

We can't deny that negative immigrant rhetoric has intensified over the past decade. While fear-mongering has long been used for political persuasion and self-gain, the rise of the internet, it seems, has given it a megaphone. News and information are at our fingertips 24/7 and can be spread with the click of a button. The problem is *it's not all true.* And it only takes one video clip, one post, or one incendiary news article to start a wildfire of anger and fear.

Regardless of whether they are confirmed facts or fabricated "facts"— the feelings they create are *real.*

What I've learned it is easier to judge, fear, or ignore others from afar. The truth is, I'll believe just about anything I'm told about someone I don't know. But when I truly *know* someone— when I have a relationship with them, when I hear their stories and see their scars— the fear melts away, and it becomes a lot harder to turn my back and ignore their needs.

Refugees, like Zinah, didn't choose where they would be born, or who their family would be. They didn't choose which government they would live under either— but every day they live with the consequences.

When Mandah met and married a man from the Middle East, she never expected it would change her life forever. They made their home in Pakistan and started a family. But Mandah was soon to discover the realities of living in such an unstable country, with frequent bombings, extreme violence, and sexism. She'll never forget one day, in particular, when some thieves came searching for anything valuable. They cut her very hand off to get to the gold bangles she was wearing. She describes the experience as "literal hell."

Imran served alongside the U.S. Army, in hopes of a brighter future for his home country of Afghanistan. He served for seven selfless years, despite immense persecution. When threats intensified, he and his wife were left with no other choice than to either dig their own graves or leave.

They arrived in America in the wake of the post-2016 election immigration debate. Despite his honorable service to the U.S., he was "rewarded" with little more than animosity and skepticism toward his brown skin.

Rafiq and his family weren't allowed to work in their own home country of Myanmar (formerly Burma). As Rohingyas, they are considered stateless, and without rights. They are treated worse than dirt. He paid $300 for a rickety boat ride he hoped would lead to a good job. What was supposed to be a five-day trip turned into ten. When they arrived in Thailand they learned the other boat travelling with them had capsized, killing over one hundred Rohingya men, women, and children. Rafiq did find work, but only after resettling in the U.S. He has spent the past three years supporting his family, halfway across the world— and holding onto hope that one day they will be reunited.

These and the other stories in this book are just a small sample of the real life experiences millions of refugees have faced and survived. The real tragedy is that their struggles don't end automatically after resettlement. Instead, they just look different.

Broken systems expect these individuals to attain early economic self-sufficiency, but don't always *empower* them to do so. Widespread xenophobia keeps them on the outskirts, and inhibits their acclimation.

> **BROKEN SYSTEMS EXPECT THESE INDIVIDUALS TO ATTAIN EARLY ECONOMIC SELF-SUFFICIENCY, BUT DON'T ALWAYS EMPOWER THEM TO DO SO.**

If we are to understand the plight of refugees better so that we can partner alongside them to help them succeed, we must first identify some common misconceptions, lean in, and find the truth.

Can just *anyone* become a refugee?

Are immigrants a threat to our safety?

How much does it cost the U.S. to resettle refugees?

Will letting them take good jobs leave enough for Americans?

These are all important questions, and some of the answers just might surprise you. Let's take a look at three widespread beliefs about refugees and refugee resettlement and see how they hold up against the facts.

Myth #1: Refugees are a terrorist threat to our country. Allowing more in will raise crime rates and put us at greater risk of attack.

Truth: Refugees are the single-most screened and vetted people group to enter the U.S. Many refugees are victims of terrorism themselves and desire to live in peace and safety. Contrary to common misconception, immigrants are far less likely to commit crimes than native-born Americans.

In our comparatively safe and stable society, it's easy to dismiss or minimize the fact that war, instability, and devastation are the daily reality for many living in other countries. Another day isn't guaranteed to any of us. But for many individuals, death from attack, starvation, and disease are an ever-present threat to their livelihood.

Zinah, from our opening story, shared this about life in Baghdad, before coming to the United States:

"The first 30 years of my life, I opened my eyes and there was war. In 2003, when the last war started, we thought it would be the end, but it just opened the doors to form many militia. There were so many terrorist groups. We woke up every morning just to hear boom, boom, boom. More people killed. They killed our professor because they didn't want academics— they wanted to keep Iraq poor and weak.

Every time I would get in my car I would have to check underneath for bombs. I was so scared, I would stop at so many traffic lights and re-check. I woke up every morning wondering if it would be the day I would die."

It wasn't until the 1970s that the United States began purposeful admission of refugees, recognizing the need to step in and help vulnerable Vietnamese after the fall of Saigon. Before this time, immigrants had come largely from European countries and nearby Cuba.[28]

Admissions became more regulated after the Refugee Act of 1980, when Congress instituted a yearly "cap" on the number allowed into the country. Programs were funded, and processes put in place to balance the safety of Americans with our desire to help those in need.

In 2001, arrivals were temporarily suspended after the infamous 9/11 attacks, which led to increased security measures. Admissions recovered, but, in the end, forever shaped the way America viewed not only Muslims, but everyone who came through our doors.

Nearly two decades later, our modern-day vetting process has developed into an intricate, multi-step, interdepartmental process wrought with red tape, designed to catch any would-be threats to our nation's security.

The refugee journey begins when a family or individual flees their home country and crosses into another. After arrival, they must file with the United Nations High Commissioner for Refugees (UNHCR) for refugee status. To qualify, the individual or family must meet UNHCR's standard definition of a refugee: "Someone who is unable or unwilling to return to their country of origin due to a well-founded fear of being persecuted for reasons of race, religion, nationality, membership of a particular social group, or political opinion."[29]

But falling within that definition doesn't guarantee resettlement. In fact, less than one percent of the world's refugees are ever resettled.[30]

> **LESS THAN ONE PERCENT OF THE WORLD'S REFUGEES ARE EVER RESETTLED.**

After collecting biographical and biometric data to establish an individual's identity, UNHCR identifies the most vulnerable cases to be referred to resettlement countries. Applicants found to have committed serious crimes are not considered for resettlement. For the few chosen to proceed, the long, grueling process of vetting is just getting started.

When entertaining the idea that terrorists could leverage refugee status to gain access into the United States, it is important to realize that refugees are *assigned* to a host country, not necessarily of their choosing.

If they're "lucky" enough to be counted among the several thousand yearly admissions to the United States, you can expect *hours* of grueling face-to-face interviews, biometric screening, and stacks of paperwork.

Not just once, but over and over again, across multiple departments, and over many unsure months of waiting. The process can take upwards of 18 to 24 months before receiving a phone call that they are cleared to enter the United States.

During this time, more than five agencies review their case, including the National Counterterrorism Center, FBI, Department of Defense, Department of Homeland Security, and Department of State.[31] If any new information, such as a former alias or any other mismatched information presents itself during this time, the process starts over. One slip of the tongue, one conflicting statement, or one inkling of malintent and the applicant's chances of being resettled dwindle even further.[*]

Refugees are vetted more extensively than any other arrivals to the United States. Our advanced technology and continuous multi-agency safeguards are so watertight that "the chance of being killed on U.S. soil in a terrorist attack committed by a refugee was 1 in 3.86 billion last year."[32]

NOT A SINGLE AMERICAN HAS BEEN KILLED BY A REFUGEE IN A TERRORIST ATTACK SINCE THE REFUGEE ACT OF 1980.

In comparison, the average American faces:

A 1 in 7 chance of dying of cancer,

A 1 in 103 chance of dying in a motor vehicle crash, and[33]

A 1 in 16,667 (approx.) chance of being a victim of homicide.[34]

The fact is *not a single American* has been killed by a refugee in a terrorist attack since the Refugee Act of 1980 and its rigorous screening procedures were put into effect .[35]

---

[*] Visit **www.refugeeworkforce.com** to watch a video interview with Malek, a Syrian refugee, about his vetting experience.

Upon deeper investigation, you will find little evidence that opening our doors to refugees, and even immigrants as a whole, poses any sort of threat to our safety. Refugees are far more likely to become victims of crime than they are to commit one, especially with our nation's recent trend in rising hate crimes fueled by negative immigrant rhetoric.

The refugees I've come to know over recent years are some of the kindest, most grateful, helpful, and generous individuals I've ever met. Which brings us to our second myth:

Myth #2: Refugees are freeloaders who hurt the economy.

Truth: Refugees are grateful contributors to society who desire to be self-sufficient.

Of all the individuals I've met, refugees are lowest on the list of people I would ever consider "freeloaders" in this country. Talk to any refugee, and you'll note a common thread of gratitude woven within every conversation.

One of the most grateful employees we've ever had was Aluet Deng, a refugee from Sudan. As a single mom with four girls, most would expect her to live out her days after resettlement in the U.S. on public assistance. Instead, she came to our Dallas office wanting a good job. After one week as part of the wait staff at Dallas Athletic Club, her supervisor told us, "Give me 20 Aluets because she's the best worker we have!"

Opportunity is so ingrained in our society that we Americans often take it for granted. I can't speak for every refugee, but the majority of those I've met are eager to grab their new life by the horns, work hard, and contribute meaningfully to society.

They view the United States not as a land of endless handouts, but as a place where, if they work hard enough for long enough, they can make a good living and a better future for their family.

Refugees are not only eager to work, they are legal to work, almost immediately. After presenting acceptable documents required for the I-9 form, they are issued Employment Authorization. Every refugee must apply for a social security number, too, which means when they work, they pay taxes just the same as you and me. (We'll see just how much, shortly.)

Let's look back at Zinah's story.

For most individuals, the ever-present threats and chaos would be reason enough to slip into survival mode.

But not for Zinah.

In the heat of the Iraq war, she obtained her bachelor's degree in biotechnology, and even began pursuing her Master's. When her parents were forced to flee and she stepped into the role of "mom" to her younger siblings, she still didn't back down from her studies.

"I was 'mom,' 'dad,' and even 'lawyer,'" she shares. "I had to put food on the table. I worked as a secretary, then a retail manager. I worked 24/7 to prove myself. Dreams are sometimes left on hold for war. In Iraq, where I came from, my life was surrounded by war. I lost almost everything before I came here, but not my dream: to be safe, and to be successful."

Zinah worked her hardest to make half of that dream come true. She was successful at just about everything she laid her hands on. So, when the opportunity came to be safe, via being resettled in the United States, she responded with an emphatic *YES*.

Would she finally relax? Would Zinah now sit back and let "the system" take care of her after all she'd done and endured in Iraq? Of course not. Zinah immediately set out to find a job. It didn't take long before others took note of her impressive drive, skill set, and accomplishments.

Within a month, Zinah landed a job at Atlanta's prestigious Emory University School of Medicine. Three years later she was suddenly laid off, but even then she didn't back down. Zinah turned the negative experience into an opportunity to go back to school, where she earned her database specialist degree, and a 3.9 GPA— all while working *and* raising her three-year-old son.

After graduating, yet again, Zinah began searching for a full-time job that would utilize her new skills. Despite *multiple* interviews ending in job offers, one stuck out to her the most— a job working with us, at Amplio Recruiting.

The opportunity to help other refugees was irresistible to Zinah who shares, "If there's something I can give, I want to give back and help our community."

Does this sound like a freeloader to you?

> "THERE IS NOTHING FOR FREE.
>
> IF YOU DON'T SWEAT, YOU DON'T EAT."

Sure, Zinah's story is just one of thousands of refugees arriving in the United States, annually. But it's a story we hear *over and over again*. While, not all refugees have prestigious degrees, they are *all* resilient, *all* grateful, and *all* eager to give back to the country opening its doors to them for safety and opportunity.[*]

Every refugee I've met was working a job to provide for their families back home, and not a single one of them expects their life to be any different here. As one of our refugee employees put it best: "There is nothing for free. If you don't sweat, you don't eat."

Okay, so refugees are eager to contribute to society. But let's address the real elephant in the room: how much does it cost to resettle each refugee? And do we receive a full return on that investment?

---

[*] Visit **www.refugeeworkforce.com** for an interview with Najib about his work, and meaningful display of gratitude to former President George W. Bush.

—

After arriving, each refugee individual or family is assigned to a resettlement agency, which gets its funding from the U.S. Department of State. The DOS allocates a modest $2,125 for each refugee arrival. However, nearly half of that ($1,000) is used to pay for the agency's services to cover their personnel and other administrative expenses.

In the end the amount received—to cover initial costs such as food and housing— boils down to a mere $1,125 per refugee. [36] A family of three, which receives $3,375, has a little more margin than a single individual relocating, who would hardly be able to afford even subsidized housing. Oh, and that's not monthly. That amount is expected to last *90 days*. And when it's gone, it's gone.

You might also be interested to learn that the cost of a refugee's flight and other transportation necessary to resettle is not paid by any program or government— it's paid by refugees and their families. Each individual receives a travel loan issued by the International Organization for Migration (IOM), which covers the cost of their flight and any other transportation in getting to their new country. Refugees are required to sign a promissory note before leaving, stating they will repay the interest-free loan in full within 42 months of resettlement.

So, adding to the pressure of starting from scratch in a new country, often with miniscule savings, and with very little assistance is this looming debt that needs to be repaid.

Now that we know how much is spent on resettling refugees in the U.S., let's look at the return on that investment. While more research has yet to be done on the economic impact of refugees in the United States, a 2017 study by the New American Economy Research Fund reported several key findings that confirm the substantial contributions the refugee community makes within the U.S. economy.

Here is what the study showed:

First, **"refugees contribute meaningfully to our economy as earners and taxpayers."**

Among the 2.3 million refugees studied, they earned a collective $77.2 billion in income, contributing $20.9 billion of that in taxes. The rest was able to be invested or spent at U.S. businesses.

Second, **"while refugees receive initial assistance upon arriving in the United States, they see particularly sharp income increases in subsequent years."** The median household income for refugees who have been in the United States for five years or less is $22,000. By the time they have lived here for 25 years, it nears $67,000, putting them *above* the average U.S. median income.

Last, **"refugees have an entrepreneurship rate that outshines even that of other immigrants."** 2015 statistics revealed:

- The percentage of native-born entrepreneurs was 9%

- The percentage of non-refugee immigrant entrepreneurs was 11.5%

- But the percentage of refugee entrepreneurs was a staggering 13%[37]

Hard workers. Business builders. Taxpayers. *Refugees.*[*]

A far cry from the charity cases or freeloaders they're often made out to be, refugees have proven they will take, and be grateful for, and make the most out of every ounce of opportunity they are given— and give back *more.*

> **HARD WORKERS.**
>
> **BUSINESS BUILDERS.**
>
> **TAXPAYERS.**
>
> **REFUGEES.**

---

[*] Visit our resource page at **www.refugeeworkforce.com** for a shareable graphic

Still, there is even more evidence revealing how refugees are not hurting, *but playing a critical part* in our current economy. Let's look at that in our third and final myth.

Myth #3: Immigrants, including refugees, are taking jobs from Americans.

Truth: As the U.S. population ages, working-age refugees are filling a critical role in combating labor shortages within the workplace.

Of all the misinformation aimed at keeping migrants out, this one is the *most* overused and *least* accurate.

There is no need to rehash everything we covered in chapter one, but I want to restate loud and clear that the overwhelming evidence within the U.S. job market indicates there is more than enough room at the table for anyone and everyone willing to work.

At the time of this writing, 7.5 *million* jobs remain unfilled in the U.S. job market.[38] Even if we filled these jobs with every individual who is currently looking for work, we're still nearly *two million* workers short of current demand. These numbers simply cannot hold. If we don't fill the already widening gap of labor shortages in our nation, there will be crippling effects to our economy.

When I started placing refugees, I had a hunch they were a viable solution to our country's labor shortage problem. Now, studies are confirming that hunch. New American Economy concluded their 2017 study with this statement: "in an era when the country faces unprecedented demographic challenges, refugees are uniquely positioned to help."

So, what makes them "uniquely positioned?"

One of the biggest factors in our crisis-level shortages is our aging population. *And it's a problem that's not going away.*

By 2050, experts project the U.S. will *double* its 65 and up population to *more than 83 million*.[39] It's obvious that very few of those will be working. This creates two primary problems: one, major shortages in "blue-collar" industries like manufacturing, which Baby Boomers previously dominated. Two, a greater need for healthcare workers to take care of the aging.

This is where we get to refugees' unique positioning.

NAE's study goes on to reveal an average of **3 out of every 4** refugee arrivals are within prime working age (25-64). That's 77%, as opposed to U.S.-born's 49%.

Of those, one out of every ten takes a job in the service industry.

One out of every seven fills a role in the healthcare industry.

And finally, the cherry on top— **one out of every five** refugees chooses to clock in at a manufacturing company.[40]

> MUCH OF THE FOOD THAT WE CONSUME, PRODUCTS WE PURCHASE, AND LUXURIES WE ENJOY WOULD NOT BE POSSIBLE WITHOUT IMMIGRANTS.

And, let's not overlook the fact that **more than 13% of refugees are creating new jobs by starting businesses.**[41]

Taking jobs *from* Americans?
More like *filling* jobs *for* Americans.

The truth is, much of the food we consume, products we purchase, and luxuries we enjoy would not be possible without immigrants, and especially the refugee workforce.

I'd say without a doubt, we can mark this myth "busted."

. . . .

Five years after being resettled, Zinah is thriving. She serves as Amplio's database manager, keeping the CRM organized, and helping track vital metrics. After five years in America, she recently became a U.S. citizen. She is now in the process of buying her first home and applying to Harvard University's PhD program for bioinformatics.

There are few individuals in this world more joyful and full of thanks than Zinah. She is grateful for the United States opening the doors for her, and her family's, safety. She is grateful she no longer has to have five locks on her front door, or check underneath her car for bombs. She is grateful she no longer has to lie in bed at night and listen to the wails from children who have lost their mom or dad.

"As refugees," Zinah shares, "we come with all this motivation because we lived through very hard times. We lived a terrible life. So when we come and see all this opportunity, we appreciate it. We want to add value. We want to give back."

Her gratitude, though, is balanced by the burden she feels for the millions of others worldwide, faced with similar circumstances, yet not given any relief.

"While I'm grateful for all I've experienced in the United States I recognize there are many displaced people who are not given the same opportunities that I've been given. I plan to make the most of these opportunities, so that I can be an example to the world of what can happen when refugees are given a chance."

. . . .

The few myths we've covered in these pages are just a drop in the bucket when it comes to all the misinformation floating around about refugees.

I hope this chapter has helped to remove any thread of doubt you may have had that refugees are not only deserving of our ongoing support, but also play an important role in the health of our economy.

We cannot remain indifferent. We must take a stance on the issue of refugee resettlement, recognizing its positive economic and social impact. Author and Iranian refugee, Dina Nayeri, wrote, "It is the obligation of every person born in a safer room to open the door when someone in danger knocks. "

Our great nation is based on the belief that people should be free to practice their religion, free from unjust government, and free to pursue limitless opportunity. Let us never take for granted what we have. Like Zinah, let us be grateful. And may that gratitude fuel us to continue being a welcoming nation, remembering where we came from and paving the way for others.

In the unforgettable words of Franklin D. Roosevelt, "Remember, remember always, that all of us, and you and I especially, are descended from immigrants and revolutionists."

Immigrants don't just need America— America needs immigrants.

In our next chapter, we'll look at the three most common hiring hindrances facing companies, and reveal why refugees are a viable solution to these challenges.

THREE | BEST-KEPT SECRET

"Now we have dependability."

Orlando Morrow has a problem: he needs *at least* twenty additional employees to get his department up to speed.

As production manager of Gourmet Foods International, he wears a lot of hats, from scheduling personnel to managing budgets— hiring is just one of those hats.

Orlando is no stranger to the task, but recently he has found himself increasingly short on qualified candidates. Limited on both time and personnel, he's tried turning to the help of traditional staffing companies. But his hopes were sorely disappointed.

"They only wanted to provide me with bodies," Morrow shares. "I was looking for long-term employees."

Employees are desperately needed to portion and package the company's popular gourmet cheeses for distribution. The position pays a decent wage, and isn't overly strenuous. Regardless, workers aren't staying.

Seven, eight, nine new hires cycle through every week, requiring hours of training. But, in the end, nearly all of them quit, and Orlando's investment of time and resources is wasted yet again.

Turnover is sky high at nearly 90%, and it is straining not only Orlando—but also his full-time employees. Productivity and morale are suffering. The team often has to clock in on weekends to meet quota, costing the company hours of overtime. Orlando's supervisor, Emile Escalera, is equally frustrated, but feels helpless to fix the problem for the struggling department.

Orlando is stumped.

Where can he turn for a viable source of dependable employees who can not only fill the gap, but also help take his department to the next level?

. . . .

When companies call our office looking to hire employees, it's remarkable to me that no matter how specific the job or unique the industry, most of them communicate the same message. Inevitably in that initial conversation about their need to fill open positions—

The furniture company needing installers,
The restaurant needing line cooks,
The police department needing patrol officers,
The golf course needing turf-techs,
The sporting goods supplier needing seamstresses,
The bakery needing oven operators,
The auto part maker needing quality assurance technicians,
The chemical plant needing compounders,
The law office needing admin assistants,
The dumpster manufacturer needing welders,
The tech firm needing data analysts,
The hospital needing sanitation stewards,
The electrical supply warehouse needing forklift drivers,
The gourmet food supplier needing cheese packagers—

Nearly every one of them will say something along the lines of, "Here is the kind of person we need for this position..."

In that moment, we grab our pen and paper to ensure we record all the details vital to placing the perfect candidate in this distinct position; but, instead of filling the page with precise qualifications we often come away with the same list:

Legal, drug-free employees who will show up on time and are willing to do the work.

It is remarkably clear the need for labor is so great that companies don't waste their time looking for top talent any more.

> THE NEED FOR LABOR IS SO GREAT THAT COMPANIES DON'T WASTE TIME LOOKING FOR TOP TALENT ANY MORE.

They've surrendered to hiring anyone who will simply show up and do the bare minimum to maintain the status quo. When we assure companies that refugees will meet and exceed the bare minimum, many remain skeptical. Maybe you're reading this and you are, too.

Maybe you've had immigrants lined up who are willing to work, but in the end, lacked the proper documentation.

Or you've had employees pass initial drug tests, only to fail several months down the line. You've experienced the frustration of having to terminate employment after investing valuable time and money into training and development.

It's likely you've spent hours scouring applications, conducting interviews, and hiring a person you *thought* would be a good employee—only for them to show up late, call in sick often, or leave to pursue another opportunity.

. . . .

While lamenting about the labor shortage struggles at Gourmet Foods to a friend one night, Emile, Orlando's supervisor, shares how he feels at a loss to help not only Orlando, but also other production managers in departments across the company.

But Daryl Shular, a Master Chef at Atlanta Athletic Club, has recently been down the same road. He shares with Emile how he has discovered new employees that are proving to be exceptionally dependable at each of his three restaurants. Then, he tells him about a unique staffing agency, connecting refugees with positions at local businesses.[*] Emile immediately texts Orlando with a link to Amplio Recruiting's website.

When Orlando receives the text, he is intrigued. He hurries home after his shift, eager to look into the promising lead.

Okay, now this is something different, Orlando thinks to himself as he scrolls the computer screen. Pursuing refugee employees was something that had never occurred to him.

At this point, he has exhausted every other hiring tactic he can think of, so he figures *why not?*

Orlando is desperate, and he even likes the philanthropic concept of opening the door of opportunity for this often overlooked people group. Still, he wonders…

Can the refugee workforce truly help his department's critical labor shortage problem?

Orlando is about to find out.

. . . .

"Why not?"

---

[*] Visit **www.refugeeworkforce.com** to see a video interview with Daryl about the Atlanta Athletic Club's experience.

This is the cry of many frustrated business owners, managers and HR reps that call our office, desperate for solutions. Even after hearing about the benefits of hiring refugees, many remain skeptical...

Can this workforce truly help our problem?
Our team is happy to respond with a confident "yes."

In the next few chapters, I'll explain how the refugee workforce can increase your company's efficiency, creativity, retention levels, and more. But for now, we're going to simply hone in on the three most essential reasons why refugees are a viable solution to your company's labor shortages.

A Legal Workforce
Legal-to-work employees are the most basic need of any company.
Since 1986, companies have been mandated to "complete and retain Form-I-9, Employment Eligibility Verification, for every person they hire for employment."[42] Verification requirements were created to deter undocumented immigrants from work, encouraging them to pursue legal routes of immigration, or return to their country of origin. Companies with improperly documented employees on their payroll can face civil or criminal penalties ranging from a few hundred dollars to a few thousand dollars for multiple offenses.

To bypass these requirements, some immigrants have simply taken to fabricating false identification, undetectable to the average eye. This is how even companies with good intentions end up hiring undocumented immigrants unknowingly.

By 1996, the U.S. government recognized this problem, and rolled out a new, optional tool for employers to authenticate their employees' legality to work. They called it E-verify.

E-verify crosschecks information provided on the I-9 form with the Social Security Administration and the Department of Homeland Security to confirm an employee's eligibility to work.

As of the writing of this book, only four states (Alabama, Arizona, Mississippi, and South Carolina) require *all* businesses to e-verify *every* employee.[43] As of now, this is the best option for company owners to protect themselves. Still, many don't.

In 2018, more than one hundred immigrants were detained by ICE agents, at Corso's Flower and Garden Center, in Ohio, for lack of proper documentation. Afterward, the company responded, in a press statement, "If mistakes were made or if anyone used false, fraudulent, or otherwise disingenuous identification documents… to secure employment at Corso's, **the company was not aware of those things**."

But ignorance isn't always bliss. Especially when it leads to a criminal investigation and thousands of dollars worth of penalties. These types of raids are only becoming more and more frequent, and the punishments more severe.

> **REFUGEES PROVIDE THE BEST OF BOTH WORLDS— A HARD-WORKING, AND LEGAL, WORKFORCE.**

Immigrant workers have long been desired in the workplace for their strong motivation, but can pose a high risk if undocumented. In industries where Americans simply aren't taking jobs, refugees provide the best of both worlds— a hard-working, *and legal,* workforce.

To understand why refugees are a safe, reliable choice for employment, let's take a look at their status within the United States' immigration system:

- All refugees are immigrants, but not all immigrants are refugees.

- Refugees are granted legal permission to be in the U.S. permanently *before* they arrive in the U.S. They do not cross the border and then request to stay legally.

- Refugees are "immigrants," different from "nonimmigrants," meaning that they intend to stay. Nonimmigrants are only allowed to stay temporarily.

We've already looked at the multi-layer vetting process that refugees endure in the months prior to resettlement in the U.S. It is because of this vetting that these individuals are fully documented and legal to work soon after arriving in America.

As ICE continues to tighten down on undocumented immigrants, refugees are quickly becoming recognized not only as a viable source of legal, but also *motivated* labor, which is the second most frequent complaint we hear from companies.

. . . .

The phone rings at Amplio Recruiting's Atlanta office. Company President Luke Keller picks up and listens to the production manager share his struggles on the other end. The situation is desperate, but not unusual these days. Orlando Morrow's department needs thirty employees to run at full capacity, yet can't seem to maintain more than ten.

"We can absolutely help you," Luke assures him. The office team begins strategically pairing qualified refugees to each job opening. There's no denying the department's main problem is turnover. Luke knows Amplio's employees can provide exactly what Gourmet needs.

This time, Orlando's hopes are not disappointed. After hiring a handful of refugees, he recognizes an immediate boost in productivity. His faith is bolstered. He hires more, inching toward his "magic number" of thirty employees.

Having workers he can count on to simply show up, and do their job day after day has changed everything. Turnover is virtually non-existent, and he no longer has to spend hours of his work week finding and training new employees. Now that he has a team he can rely on, Orlando can focus on getting to know his team, and other important tasks.

Everyone is grateful. The company's new refugee employees are grateful for the opportunity to work, and Orlando's team is grateful for the relief they have brought.

"Hiring refugees has impacted my department greatly," Orlando shares with gratitude. "We have built our workforce. Now, we have dependability."

. . . .

A Dependable Workforce

Beyond documented workers, companies need employees who will show up, on time, ready to work. At Amplio, we simply call this responsibility. Responsibility over time equals dependability.

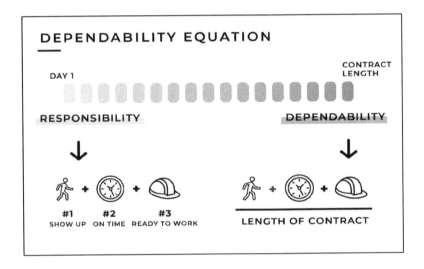

Dependability is the most supreme value of the refugee workforce.

We often hear from companies that the people they have hired in the past don't seem interested in putting in a hard day's work for a fair wage, and are ready to jump ship at the next opportunity that comes along— refugees show up, work hard, and they *stay*.

We'll look more closely at the motivating factors behind this in our next chapter, but the dependability of the refugee workforce is how clients like Gourmet Foods International have finally been able to gain traction, instead of spending precious time, energy, and resources into constant hiring, training, and rehiring. For many, the difference is extreme. Orlando's department went from a mere ten employees to fully staffed and able to meet production without incurring overtime.

> **DEPENDABILITY IS THE MOST SUPREME VALUE OF THE REFUGEE WORKFORCE.**

Showing up on time and working hard are attributes companies can no longer take for granted. In a day and age when quitting is common, it is *less common* for refugees. An impressive 73% of interviewed companies employing refugees reported higher retention rates among their refugee employees.[44]

One factor contributing to this high dependability is the refugee community's nearly non-existent rates of substance abuse, which meets another growing need of U.S. companies.

A Drug-free Workforce
Legal. Dependable. Drug-free.

It should be obvious by now that the bar has been set pretty low, and yet many Americans just aren't reaching it. More and more drug tests are coming back positive. Drug usage and addiction seem more widespread and socially acceptable than ever before.

I mentioned in chapter one that many companies have become so desperate, they've lowered the bar even further. A report from USA Today revealed, "A growing share of employers waive pre-employment drug tests or overlook positive results, especially for marijuana, amid the spread of legalized pot and a tight labor market that's making it harder to find qualified workers."[45]

As a staffing professional, there are two major problems with this trend that shakes me to the core:

First, safety should be a top priority for every company, *especially* safety-sensitive workplaces with high workers compensation insurance coverage. Work environments involving heights and heavy machinery necessitate assiduous and alert workers to protect, first, their employees, but also their assets.

Second, even in work spaces where safety isn't a blatant concern, studies show that drug-free workplaces are happier, healthier and more efficient than those that are not.[46] The cost of substance abuse isn't always lives, it can be company morale and high turnover. One Florida construction company, totaling approximately 150 laborers, estimated they lose $57,386 annually due to employee substance abuse which causes rapid turnover, wasted time, stolen goods, and high healthcare costs.[47]

In other words: employees who use drugs pose a high risk, and present very low motivation.

As more Americans fall by the wayside, passing drug tests is simply another non-problem area when it comes to refugees. In Erie, Pennsylvania, opioid usage has become an epidemic. Local manufacturer, Sterling Technologies, was just one of many companies struggling to find workers who could pass their mandatory drug test. They decided to try a different approach: hiring newly resettled refugees. Since then, every single refugee has passed not only the initial drug test, but also their ongoing screenings.

While there is very little information available on the prevalence of substance abuse among the refugee community in particular, a 2016 study, published by the University of Minnesota, revealed immigrants, in general, have lower rates of substance abuse disorders than U.S.-born citizens.[48] As one of Sterling's refugee employees shared, "In our lives, we don't have drugs."[49]

Like Sterling Technologies, drug testing is a mandatory part of the pre-screening process at Amplio— and our results have been the same. Since we opened in 2014 up until the publishing of this book, we have yet to have even one refugee applicant fail a drug test.

Let me reiterate— **of the several thousands of refugees who have walked through our doors, in cities across the country, ZERO have tested positive for drug usage.**

That's pretty remarkable, if you ask me.

Current Workforce Options
Let's track backward to that burning question Orlando Morrow had, and that many business leaders are currently asking: *Where can I find legal, drug-free employees who will show up on time and do the work?*

If you're tracking with me this far, then the following 2 x 2 diagram plotting the three choices American companies currently have when it comes to hiring should be logical:

In the top-left box, the "disappearing workforce" represents American-born individuals whom, based on the data, have vacated their position from the top-right (legal & motivated) box. As we discussed in chapter one, there are multiple contributing factors here, but one is worth repeating: a staggering 47% of unemployed males cited disability as their reason for unemployment. Over the past decade, they have become a largely unmotivated, and quickly dwindling workforce.

The bottom-right box identifies individuals who are willing and able to work but who are not legally allowed to participate in the marketplace due to their place of birth being outside the US or not having obtained the proper legal immigration status to have the right to work in America.

At this time, hiring these individuals poses high risk to any company. All that needs to be said here is that how we handle those already in the U.S. compared to those wishing to illegally cross the border at some point in the future are two very separate issues. I strongly believe undocumented immigrants living in the US who can demonstrate a strong work ethic and an intention to pay taxes—who will have an immediate positive impact on our nation's economy and their local communities— should be granted permanent status. Every American should have a strong understanding of the economic impact of immigration policy for both of these groups before jumping to any conclusions.

Finally, the top-right box depicts the central argument of this book in revealing the refugee workforce as an American company's best option for legal and motivated employees. I am not attempting to say there are no motivated Americans or that there are no impediments in hiring refugees (which we will cover in the next section), but I am hopefully articulating the shift from the workforce of "Industrial Age America" to the reality of the current workforce at our disposal.[*]

---

[*] For more on industrial age employment practices, download a free PDF of "Why Employees are Always a Bad Idea," by Chuck Blakeman, from our book website at **www.refugeeworkforce.com**.

The best kept secret for the future of the American economy should no longer be a secret to you: legal and motivated refugees.

Barriers vs. Hurdles

At this point you might be thinking, "Chris, if refugees make such great employees, then why aren't more companies pursuing them?" I believe there are several factors. We call them "hurdles." While barriers prevent hiring altogether, we've found hurdles can be overcome with a little forethought and a lot of communication.

Hurdles work both ways, keeping refugees from careers that would utilize their fullest potential, while at the same time keeping businesses from actively engaging the refugee community for employment.

It would be careless for us to paint a flawless picture of the ease of hiring refugees. The reality is, when integrating refugees into any workplace, there *will* be challenges— for refugee and company alike.

In my five years of experience, I've seen my refugee neighbors navigate these hurdles just like they've overcome so many larger obstacles in their past: with perseverance and grace. At the same time, I've seen passionately determined companies step in and find ways to lower these hurdles for their refugee employees.

Let's look at a few of the most common challenges, and some examples of how our clients have approached them.

Language Proficiency

The first question we are often asked, when companies are on the verge of hiring refugees, boils down to this: *How well do they speak English?*

While some refugees arrive fully proficient in the English language, many more do not. At Amplio, we rank every job applicant on a 1-5 scale when they first arrive at our office. Some companies prefer to hire only individuals fluent in English (fives), while others have created environments where those who haven't fully mastered the language can flourish (ones through fours).

Many have recognized a valuable truth: just because someone is not yet fluent in English does not mean they lack intelligence. In fact, they may already speak *several* other languages.

An employee who packages product and understands very little English isn't any less capable than one who is fluent. **A lack of English proficiency doesn't negate a person's experience, education, or enthusiasm.** The refugee journey develops perseverance and problem-solving skills— a survivor who has navigated their way safely across the globe with very little help can certainly handle a task that is demonstrated in front of them.

> JUST BECAUSE SOMEONE IS NOT FLUENT IN ENGLISH DOES NOT MEAN THEY LACK INTELLIGENCE. IN FACT, THEY MAY ALREADY SPEAK SEVERAL OTHER LANGUAGES.

Something we've noticed is that non-fluent individuals learn English fastest once they're in a job. English courses are great, but nothing expedites knowledge of another language like hearing it spoken for hours at a time and being expected to communicate using it.

Most refugees I meet have a strong desire to learn the English language, and employers can play a huge role. Some companies we've connected with, like Storr Office Environments in Raleigh, and Weighted Comforts in Nashville, have begun offering on-site ESL (English as a Second Language) classes— sometimes even on company time.

While in ESL classes alone, we see slow English improvement and in a job alone we see job-specific vocabulary development, put the two experiences together and we see very rapid English improvement (see visual on the following page).

Limited language proficiency can, however, complicate communication. But here are a few things to consider:

First of all, demonstrations are very powerful.

The majority of refugees I've met have an insatiable desire to learn more and perform to very high standards (we'll look more into this in our chapter 5 about growth mindset).

Second, a picture is worth a thousand words. In positions where quality assurance is vital, many employers have placed pictures in visible areas to show what a product is supposed to look like, or demonstrate potential defects.

Lastly, placing one high-fluency employee can build a bridge for other, less fluent individuals to succeed. When filling multiple positions at a company, we often place an English proficient employee first, we call them bridge builders, who is then able to help other less proficient individuals along the way. This method has had a tremendous impact in the communities we serve.

We'll share Mohammad Soda's story later, who played a huge role in building a bridge for other refugees to join the team at Gourmet International.

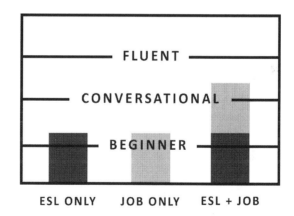

Transportation

After language fluency, the second question we're most often asked is in regards to transportation. *"Do they have a car? If not, how will they get to work?"*

Approximately 60 percent of job applicants in our offices have their own vehicle, compared to the national average of over 90 percent.[50] Despite this fact, we have yet to see the lack of owning personal transportation keep an employee from a job.

The bottom line is this: the refugee workforce is motivated, and will find a way to get to work. Bus, taxi, train, carpool, biking and walking are all modes of transportation used daily by our employees to get to their jobs.

Take for example Claudy, a young man from the Democratic Republic of Congo, who was placed at a landscaping company. After one month on the job, our Raleigh managing director discovered that Claudy was running the 5.8 miles *each way* to work while he saved up for a car. *Keep in mind that was on top of the energy he was exerting at work, in the heat of summer.* In Claudy's case, we helped him get a bicycle, to reduce his commute time and ensure enough energy to put in a hard day's work.

Another great example is Deen, a refugee from Afghanistan, who moved to the U.S. less than a year ago. We had the joy of placing him in his first job at a manufacturing company, about six months ago. Since then, he's been working hard and saving for a car, which he will finally be able to purchase later this month. Last Friday, a shipment was delayed, and he was told to take the day off, since there would be no work. But to everyone's surprise, the shipment ended up arriving on time. The company called Deen and asked if he was available to come in to work, after all.

Since Deen is still learning English, they called our office as well, to make sure Deen knew he could come in to work if he was available. When Yonten, one of our team members, called Deen, he answered sounding out of breath. *Yonten was alarmed.* He asked if Deen was okay, to which he replied, "Oh yes! I am running to work!" Even at 47 years old, he knew he could make the 2-mile trek to work faster than if he waited for the bus.

We've also seen companies approach transportation in innovative ways. When AGRO Merchants, a global food storage company, recognized the benefits of hiring refugees, they decided it was worth the investment of initially paying for transportation for three months, to get the right employees to their warehouse in Savannah, Georgia.

> **20% OF OUR EMPLOYEES PURCHASE A CAR WITHIN THEIR FIRST THREE MONTHS OF EMPLOYMENT.**

Even if a refugee doesn't own a personal vehicle, many possess a valid driver's license. Canopy Lawn Care recognized this and strategically assigned company trucks, along with the responsibility of picking up other workers, to some of their refugee employees with licenses.

Let's not overlook the fact that a job is what affords these individuals the opportunity to eventually save, or build enough credit, to secure personal transportation. We'll look at this more in chapter seven, but an interesting stat is that 20% of our employees purchase a car within their first three months of employment.

In short, transportation is a very low hurdle to clear.

Cultural Differences

From culture to culture, job etiquette and communication styles vary greatly. We have found this is one of the most difficult hurdles that can trip up many otherwise great employer-employee relationships, causing them to fail. I've seen small misunderstandings—on everything from time-off policies to appropriate restroom usage—nearly cost employees their jobs.

There are several keys we've found to evade unnecessary contention:

- **Slow onboarding time.** What you would typically cover in two days, with a traditional employee, spread it out over a week or so. It's better to over-communicate on the front-end than have to make amends for lost time, resources and relationships on the back-end.

- **Don't leave anything to chance.** Communicate, communicate, communicate. Be direct with instruction and don't assume the other person immediately understands. Overstate tasks and ask questions to assess comprehension. Avoid demeaning tones and be patient with questions, and don't assume employees understand even the most basic cultural norms.

- **Understand honor-shame culture.** While the Western world generally operates under a "guilt-innocence culture," a different culture dominates much of the Eastern world: honor-shame. While an American employee may ask (verbally, or with their actions), "Is what I do acceptable?" individuals from honor-shame cultures ask, "Is who I am acceptable?"

  It is crucial to acknowledge this difference in order to understand seemingly bizarre behavior and response. For instance, someone from an honor-shame culture would rather not show up at all than to be late and embarrass (shame) his or herself. On the flip-side, they will do all that is asked of them and work harder than the average employee to bring honor to themselves, their families, and their community.

- **Praise publicly and challenge privately.**
  In light of this honor-shame culture, it's important to remember that while correction is necessary, shame is optional.

  When dealing with conflict, undone or incorrect tasks, and other workplace actions, it is of utmost importance to protect the honor of your employee. This is best done privately.

  Oppositely, when you recognize an employee performing their duties, going above and beyond, taking ownership, and exhibiting growth— praise them publicly.

Take the time to commend them in front of their peers. This will go a long way in your relationship. An employee who feels valued will be a productive and loyal team member.

- **Promote inclusivity.**
  We'll dive deeper into this in Chapter six, but for now I'll just say that every human being has the same desire— to belong. Assess your company's culture— is it welcoming and inclusive to everyone?[*]

Education & Pertinent Work Experience

Many refugees have years of meaningful work experiences, that may or may not translate to the American workplace. The same goes for education, degrees, and certifications. Many refugees are left to start over in their careers after resettlement.

I'm a firm believer that this discrepancy should not disqualify refugees from jobs they are more than capable of executing. As I've made clear before, refugees' motivation and resilience make them eager students in any position they fill.

Thorough on-the-job training is all that many need to bridge the gap between an individual's knowledge and experience, and what they need to know to get the job done. In the case of manufacturing, the work may be familiar, but the technology vastly different from what an individual experienced in their country of origin. Higher safety standards and advanced machinery may require some upskilling, a challenge refugees are more than willing to take on. Just ask Engent Inc. in Atlanta. When filling a quality assurance position, they wanted someone detail-oriented and technologically fluent. We sent Robe, an Ethiopian immigrant with a degree in secretary science and office management, years of computer experience, and— most importantly, *a passion to grow.*

---

[*] We provide consulting services to companies across the country, and this is always the most sought after information. For more information on creating an environment that attracts and retains refugee talent, check out the consulting page on our **website**.

Her job would be to confirm the successful installation of electronic microchip processors, post-production. After an interview, the company expressed strong concerns that Robe would not be a good fit, but gave her the opportunity to prove herself. During her first week of training, the company was so impressed with her attention to detail and intuitive questions that they allowed her to jump right into the position on her own, something that usually took a month or more with previous hires in the role.

Robe is a testament that capacity must be determined by more than a resume or certificate— it is proven by grit and a growth mindset. When it comes to concerns about pertinent education and work experience, the bottom line is this: don't disqualify a person solely on lack of relevant experience. In doing so, you may be passing up some of the very best candidates.

> **REFUGEES ARE QUICKLY BECOMING AMERICA'S MOST SOUGHT-AFTER WORKFORCE.**

Conclusion

In this chapter we've learned how refugees meet three very basic, but crucial, needs within the American workplace. We've looked at the three hiring options, and seen how refugees are America's best-kept secret for the future health of our economy. We recognized common hurdles keeping refugees from fully engaging in the workplace, and learned some ways companies can lower them to gain a dependable workforce.

But beyond just being uniquely positioned to fill growing labor shortages, refugees make exemplary employees— so much so that companies from Gourmet Foods International to Starbucks are *intentionally seeking them out.*[51] In the coming chapters, we'll look at their appealing attributes and see why refugees are quickly becoming America's most sought-after workforce.

FOUR | FLAT TIRES

"When you work hard, everything becomes easy."

Mohammad Soda's alarm wakes him out of a deep slumber. The sun is not even up when he wills himself out of bed to get ready for the long day ahead.

The sound stirs his six-year-old brother, who rolls over and promptly falls back to sleep. Mohammad dresses, and crams his heavy school books into an overburdened backpack.

After a hearty breakfast, he bids "ma' al-salāmah," *"with peace,"* to his mom and heads out to catch the bus. In a few more months, these early mornings will pay off. He'll finally have his GED, the first step toward his dream of becoming a doctor.

On the college campus, you would never know Mohammad didn't speak any English just seven months prior. Or that his education came to an abrupt stop more than three years ago.

He never did anything to deserve the war that beset his beloved nation of Syria, but Mohammad is determined not to allow it to continue holding him back. He keeps pace with his classmates, listening intently and asking questions.

. . . .

In the first section of this book, we've laid a strong foundation for understanding the realities of both the current US job market, and the plight of refugees. We learned how these two problems, when put together, can serve as an economically sound solution to each other.

So far, you've met resilient individuals like Zinah and Mohammad, who represent the very best of what the refugee community has to offer. You've also met companies like Gourmet Foods International that recognized the value of hiring the refugee workforce and have experienced incredible outcomes.

Are these isolated instances, or is there a formula to their success?

While each company's journey in hiring refugees varies to some degree, we believe there is a common pattern— a cycle, actually, that when set into motion yields both company and employee growth. To better understand this success, let's first take a look at where many American companies are finding themselves stuck.

The "Flat Tire"

If you're a business owner or manager with employees, you've probably experienced this frustration: you work hard, and do everything within your power to propel your company forward every day. You've invested time and money on strategic marketing, product development, and supply chain management. But, in the end, the payoff isn't what you hoped.

You're left feeling disappointed and frustrated because your company isn't moving forward at the speed you expected, or, *at all.*

The problem is you have a "flat tire." And, like any bike with a flat tire, the owner has to put in *more* effort for *less* result.

The problem isn't your lack of skill or ambition— it's your lack of a dependable workforce.

Like many companies, you took for granted there would be plenty of people willing to put in an honest day's work for a good wage. You thought if you offered adequate pay, and intentional leadership, your team would meet every production goal and business would soar. *However, this hasn't proven to be the case.*

No matter how hard you pedal, the lack of a dependable workforce is like a flat tire, keeping you from making much progress. Without workers who will show up on time and take responsibility for their duties, you're stuck in an exhausting cycle of hiring, micromanaging, and rehiring.

When I first began placing refugees, I knew two things: First, there was a great need for dependable workers and, second, refugees were great candidates to fill this need. Since this time, I've heard testimony after testimony proving this belief to be true. I've seen some of the worst "flat tires" repaired as companies have engaged the refugee workforce.

> **WITHOUT WORKERS WHO WILL SHOW UP ON TIME AND TAKE RESPONSIBILITY FOR THEIR DUTIES, YOU'RE STUCK IN AN EXHAUSTING CYCLE OF HIRING, MICROMANAGING, AND REHIRING.**

When sharing their stories, they say things like—

"Our productivity went up."

"We were finally able to achieve consistency."

"Our turnover dropped."

"The level of effort they bring is fantastic."

"We got way more than hard work, we got better strategy and problem-solving."

Look closely at their stories and a pattern emerges. A healthy cycle of mutual effort and investment on behalf of both employer and employee.

Let's take a look at this new cycle, when "flat tires" are repaired by hiring from within the refugee workforce.

Motivation to Hire | Motivation to work
The cycle begins when an employer experiences a need for dependable employees. With over 7.5 million current job openings, at the time of this writing, this "motivation to hire" represents a vast majority of U.S. businesses. One of these is Compac Industries, in Atlanta.

Compac Industries is a leading baby product manufacturer making everything from baby toothbrushes to pacifier clips. When I first met with their leadership team, they had recently moved into a larger warehouse to accommodate their growing inventory needs— now, they needed more team members.

While the president of the company, Dean-Paul Hart, shared they had "a strong number of American workers," he described the rest as "a revolving door... who wouldn't show up for shifts that start at living wage."[52] They even created an inviting and comfortable work area for their newly anticipated employees, but had no one to enjoy it. They tried everything from running ads in the local paper, to posting online, but still remained short-handed, with very few applicants.

Many companies in similar situations turn to traditional staffing, and unknowingly prolong the "flat tire" cycle with their temporary team of uncommitted workers. Remember how Orlando Morrow described his experience with traditional staffing? "They only wanted to provide [him] with bodies." Fortunately, in Dean-Paul's case, he heard about Amplio and decided to take a chance on the refugee workforce.

The figure on the next page represents companies who take this different approach, and hire a refugee who is equally *(if not more)* motivated to work than the company is motivated to fill their open position. Joined together by their mutual need, the employer is represented by the front tire, and the refugee employee is represented by the back.

Starting with motivation, each section in between spokes on the employer (front) tire correlates to the same section on the refugee employee (back) tire. Let me explain how we see the cycle often play out.

It's easy to understand the company's motivation, given the tremendous need for workers we covered in chapter one. But let's take a moment to look at the refugee employee's motivation, and why it is often greater than that of their American-born counterparts.

A 2017 report from the Migration Policy Institute revealed "refugee men are more likely to work than U.S.-born men, while refugee women work at the same rate as their U.S.-born counterparts."[53] The reason behind their motivation is not complicated: after being forced to start life over again, refugees are driven by their desire to regain some sense of the life—*and dignity*— taken from them.

Starting over is a daunting task, as there are three primary areas they must re-establish: career, capital, and community.

For now, we'll look at the first two.

With limited financial assistance, the race to secure income begins the moment their plane touches down in the United States. Adding to that stress is the reality of navigating an unfamiliar employment process— *in a language many are just beginning to learn.*

We cannot emphasize enough the fact that the vast majority of refugees already had steady and successful careers before fleeing, but refugees who are new to the English language often struggle to articulate their prior skills and experience effectively.

The other unfortunate reality is many of these careers don't carry over into the American marketplace. Refugees like Zinah, who we met in chapter two, have to completely change fields in order to gain some forward momentum. As one individual best described it, to refugees, USA stands for 'You (U) Start Again."[54]

Re-establishing capital is another motivating factor behind the desire to work. Many refugees have had little or no access to work for months, or even years, prior to resettlement. With no credit history, and often no savings safety net, financial security is a priority.

As the clock ticks and their dollars dwindle, it's no wonder many refugees end up taking jobs for which they are grossly overqualified. But this doesn't seem to deter them from putting in 110% effort in any role they fill.

Work Ethic | Productivity
That brings us to stage two of the cycle. Because of their high motivation, the vast majority of refugees possess an unparalleled work ethic. It's what empowers individuals like Mohammad and Zinah to work one or more jobs, care for their families, and pursue higher education— and surpass others while doing it. As Mohammad Soda told me after his first few weeks on the job, "When you work hard, everything else becomes easy."[*]

---

[*] Download a sharable graphic of Mohammad's quote at **www.refugeeworkforce.com**

This strong work ethic results in an obvious benefit for companies: higher productivity. Remember Orlando's story? After filling his department's open positions with the refugee workforce, productivity went from an estimated 30% to 90%, dramatically reducing the need for overtime. Everyone felt the relief. His permanent workers were no longer having to pick up the slack for unmotivated "help," and Orlando could focus more on improving business than on filling positions due to constant turnover.

> **THEIR PRODUCTION TRIPLED, NOW THAT THEIR "FLAT TIRE" WAS REPAIRED.**

Another great example comes from Compac, the baby product manufacturer. In our first week staffing for them, we took four women for an interview: Nigh, Cing, and Nwae Nwae from Burma, and Sudad from Iraq. Compac hired them all. Based on previous performance, the expected daily quota for manufacturing pacifier clips was 300.

After just a few weeks experience, the four new employees were consistently making 600-900 clips per day without sacrificing at all on quality. Another Burmese woman, Damcey, who was hired shortly thereafter, once produced *1,100 clips in one day*. All this happened while chatting, laughing, singing along to music on their boombox, and rolling around in their comfy office chairs.

Everyone was amazed, but especially the leadership at Compac. Their production tripled, now that their "flat tire" was repaired.

This is the point of the cycle where the rubber meets the road, and we see the greatest divergence between successful and unsuccessful hires. Some companies are elated by their newfound productivity, but take no initiative to repay their workers' efforts by reinvesting in them. Other companies recognize and appreciate these changes, and take intentional steps to further integrate their refugee employees.

This takes us to stage three of our cycle.

Greater Integration | Gratitude + Welcome
In a collaborative study on Refugee Integration in the Workplace, the Tent Partnership for Refugees and Deloitte concluded integration is key when it comes to "maximizing business benefits [of hiring refugees]."[55]

Integration goes further than just lowering the "hurdles" to employment we discussed in chapter three (although that is a great start). True integration creates a sense of belonging that lets refugee employees know they are more than just a cog in the machine of productivity—they are welcomed and valued, and their employers care about their success. As Tent/Deloitte explains, "Successful workplace integration creates an environment where refugees are enabled to thrive and use their skills to their full potential."[56]

Integration begins with **acknowledgement** and **acceptance** of cultural differences. Many companies are only successful at *tolerating* differences. But integration requires that we recognize and embrace them. Deloitte describes the power of an integrated workplace: "In a successfully integrated workplace, *all employees can bring their authentic selves to work.*" This may sound hokey to you, but research shows it directly impacts the bottom line. Going out of the way to engage with employees, and learn more about who they are, where they're from, and what they like or dislike communicates value and acceptance.

When it comes to integration, leadership is key. "Strong messaging from employer leadership on the importance of accepting all employees and supporting workplace integration is critical to its success. This brings all employees on board in realizing that everyone has a role to play in making sure new employees are integrated into the workplace."[57]

When Dean-Paul first hired refugees at Compac, he shares many of their American-born workers "had questions about the newcomers' differences and where they were coming from." To that, he answered, "Let's get beyond the name; let's get beyond the language."[58]

In addition to acknowledgement and acceptance, companies who experience the highest levels of success are the ones that take steps to **accommodate** their refugee employees' differences.

Ignoring cultural differences doesn't work. The truth is, hiring employees from varying backgrounds and beliefs may require going back to the drawing board to add to or assess current company programs, policies, hiring practices, and traditions.

When Karen Hall, Vice President of HR at Gates Corporation, in Atlanta, heard about the opportunity to hire refugees, she made a bold move. Instead of interviewing only licensed forklift drivers for their open warehouse positions, Karen developed a plan with us to hire refugee employees for their entry-level warehouse positions. Then, after three months of proving their dependability, these individuals would be eligible to train on the forklift.

Daywoe, a joyful Liberian with a wife and two children, was our first temp-to-perm placement at Gates. Though he had lived in the United States for over a decade, this job was the first to give him and his family the financial stability they needed to flourish.

After three months on the job, he was hired on as a permanent employee and given the opportunity for forklift training, along with health benefits and a higher pay. Daywoe was finally able to purchase a reliable car, and even put a down payment on a house for his family.

"He took in everything the supervisors gave him in order to be successful," Karen shared. "His performance is excellent. Daywoe works so hard to get up to speed on production, and is very conscientious." Gates' story, among others, are evidence that small shifts to accommodate non-traditional new-hires can yield favorable results for both employer and employee.

Here are some questions we encourage companies to ask in assessing how "accommodating" their work environment may be:

- Are safety and other relevant signs posted in the native languages of employees to assure full understanding of a safe environment?

- Do you have an intra-company multicultural calendar to avoid scheduling important events or meetings on major cultural holidays?

- In the onboarding process, are materials offered in both English and the employee's native language?[*]

- Are meet-and-greets, building tours, team lunches, and other activities in place to ease the new employee into a comfortable atmosphere?

- Are training materials or presentations reviewed before introducing them to employees of different cultures to see if anything needs to be modified or explained in a different way?

- Do you offer a list and description of local resources that may help refugee employees such as bus routes and convenient ESL classes?

Accommodation doesn't have to mean foregoing your company's favorite fourth of July picnic, or giving your Muslim employees the entire month of Ramadan off. But it does mean approaching these situations through the lens of *all* employees, *and being flexible.*

Considerations can be as simple as swapping grilled hotdogs for a potluck-style celebration, or introducing a "floating paid holiday schedule."

---

[*] For help with translating employee handbooks and office materials, we recommend partnering with Voxy (**www.voxy.com**). Voxy takes a unique approach in helping both companies and new American employees remove the language hurdle to promote successful careers.

Think of accommodation as an equalizer. Deloitte's integration study found when companies invest in creating a more "equitable work environment," they experience "a more inclusive, connected, and productive workplace" that is beneficial not just to refugees, but to *all*.[59]

The third and final component of an inclusive workplace is **appreciation**. Deloitte explains this succinctly:

"For some refugees in the U.S., a first job— or an entire career— may not be a 'dream job' or the best match to their skills. This makes it... important for refugees to find purpose in their work and feel a part of something greater..."

Frequent affirmation assures employees their work matters. When they know their skills and contributions are needed, they feel a deep sense of purpose no matter the work.

> **ALL OF THESE INVESTMENTS COMMUNICATE ONE KEY THING: WELCOME.**

Acknowledgement and acceptance.
Accommodation.
Appreciation.

This phase of the cycle is really the key to unlocking the fullest potential of the refugee workforce. Why? Because all of these investments communicate one key thing: **welcome.**

In a study of 26 companies, the Tent Partnership for Refugees found, "All workers value employers who made them feel welcome and respected, but refugees are especially responsive to a welcoming environment."[60]

Hamdi Ulukaya, CEO of Chobani, has set a strong pace in the corporate world when it comes to creating a welcoming environment for employees. His highly successful Greek yogurt company is comprised of *30% refugee and immigrant employees.* He shared with The New York Times, "If you want to build a company that truly welcomes people—including refugees—one thing you have to do is throw out this notion of 'cheap labor.' That's really awful. They're not a different group of people, they're not Africans or Asians or Nepalis. They're each just another team member. Let people be themselves, and if you have a cultural environment that welcomes everyone for who they are, it just works."[61]

Welcome is not something refugees take for granted. Many have experienced heart-wrenching rejection by their countries, their governments, or even their families because of who they are, where they were born, or what they believe. So to have a community open their arms in welcome is incredibly meaningful to them, and they are grateful.

"Refugees are dying to provide for their community," Hamdi concludes. "I always said that the minute they got the job, that's the minute they stopped being refugees."

But that gratitude isn't the end of the road. Instead, it serves as fuel for the next stage in our cycle, which leads to another big benefit for companies.

Loyalty | High Retention + Recruitment
We're now more than halfway through our cycle, and here's where things start to pick up momentum. This is also where the biggest difference between the refugee workforce and other employees starts to take shape:

Refugees who feel welcomed are grateful.
Their gratitude makes them loyal.
Their loyalty causes them to stay longer, and recruit others.

In the last chapter, we talked about the dependability of the refugee workforce: they show up, on time, and work hard. Loyalty goes even a step beyond that. Their gratitude for a positive, welcoming work environment compels them to stay longer. In a study by the Tent Partnership for Refugees, researchers found rates of turnover among refugee employees were "7 to 15 percentage points lower than for the overall workforce". In their interviews with 26 employers across several industries, 19 firms reported lower turnover rates for their refugee employees, when compared to other employees.[62]

In our experience, the industry standard for retention after three months sits at a dismal 40%. After five years of repairing "flat tires" for local companies, we are seeing an 80% retention rate after 3 months, and nearly 70% after an entire year.

Rafi, from Afghanistan, has worked at Engent (electronic manufacturing) for over three years and is now a Department Leader.

Poh, from Burma, has worked his way from Pipefitting Apprentice to Team Leader, after two years at Fire and Life Safety Services.

Karimi, also from Afghanistan, has put in over two years at R James Properties and worked his way up to the role of Maintenance Director.[*]

Mohammad, from Iran, has been with the Atlanta Athletic Club for over two years, and is now a Kitchen Leader.

But beyond higher retention, the study also concluded that a refugee's loyalty pays in *recruitment* of more refugees. Simply put: refugees who feel welcomed like to talk about it. And companies that have learned to nurture an inclusive workplace have already set the stage for successful integration of these new recruits.

---

[*] Visit **www.refugeeworkforce.com** to watch an interview with Karimi.

Rafi, Poh, Karimi and Mohammad have not only been faithful and been given more responsibility, but each of them have been responsible for multiple hires at their respective companies from their own social network.

It's easy to see an increase in retention will result in a decrease in money spent recruiting, onboarding, and training. Compile this with motivated employees, and you get an overall more productive environment.

Increased Profit + Revenue | More Opportunity
With steady productivity growth comes another increase: this time, in profit. The combination of less turnover, plus more units being produced, and customers served by the same number of employees, causes the bottom line to soar.

Let's take Compac, for example. Previously, if they needed to produce 1,200 units to fill an order, and their quota was 300 units, they would have to expense four workers at eight hours to fill the order. After hiring a handful of refugee employees, they saw productivity increase to the point where they only needed to expense four people at four hours to fill the order (or even two people at eight hours), because they were consistently producing 600 units per day. This change effectively cut their labor costs in half!

Higher productivity without paying higher labor costs has a massive positive impact on the bottom line.

As companies engage the refugee workforce, retention begins to stabilize. Productivity and profit increase. Everyone takes notice of the difference—but particularly, the sales team. At this point it's likely they're seeing a surplus of inventory begin to stock up, and they can eagerly sell as opposed to constantly backfilling orders and crossing their fingers that deadlines will be met. As the sales team's confidence in their company's capacity to fill orders surges, they can sell more and win bigger contracts, leading to an increase in revenue.

After months or years of being stuck in the same "flat tire" cycle, the company finally has traction— now, it's the employer who is grateful. Increased profit and revenue make way for them to invest back in the business — and back into those whose hard work got them here.

At this point, companies can begin to consider ways to help their refugee employees move beyond integration to advancement. Many offer skills training, leadership training, ESL classes or scholarships to attain higher education. As companies demonstrate this faith in their employees' potential, those employees experience a new level of dignity in their abilities and contributions. This leads us to the final phase before the cycle revolves again.

Dignity | Greater Demand

Now, both the company and refugee employees are experiencing growth. Winning bigger contracts means the company will now need to hire more employees, and at this point they can't imagine looking anywhere other than the refugee workforce.

Some companies, like Compac, have experienced this in as little as a few short weeks. After initially hiring four refugees, and tripling production, they began to land even larger contracts, and immediately hired more.

As for refugee employees, reclaiming dignity is nothing short of powerful. At Amplio, we have a front row seat to the dignity and worth coming from engaging in work. Many individuals come into our office, initially, with their heads down and shoulders slumped. After being placed, they return to pick up paychecks with smiles on their faces and heads held high.

We hear dignity woven into their statements—

"Before I got this job, I was struggling to help my mom. Now, I can take care of my family."

"I just wanted to get back to work. I hadn't worked [for months]. To have a job a few minutes from my home— paying bills, having benefits, keeping food on the table and a roof on my head— I am very happy."

"In the first four or five months after coming here, I felt like I may have made a mistake. Now, I have a bright hope."

We'll discuss the power of dignity more in a later chapter, but at this point, the refugee employee becomes motivated to work even harder, climb the ladder of opportunity, and invite others to join them.

> **COMPANIES INVEST IN EMPLOYEES.**
>
> **EMPLOYEES INVEST IN THE COMPANY.**
>
> **EVERYBODY MOVES FORWARD.**

The cycle repeats:
Companies invest in employees.
Employees invest in the company.
Everybody moves forward.

This is the point where we see another attribute of the Refugee Workforce begin to *shine.*

We've talked about refugees' resilience— their determination to get back up after a life-altering blow. We've discovered how gratitude motivates them to give back to their communities, and their country. We've acknowledged their undeniably strong work ethic and loyalty.

Could there really be more?

As it turns out, there is. Once refugees are finally able to move out of survival mode, it seems they shift into a new mindset, where all limits are off. They recognize there is no end to the opportunity— if they work hard, they can achieve their goals. If there's something they don't know how to do, they figure out how to do it. They take critique and turn it into action. They pursue every ounce of training, advice, and information they can get their hands on.

Sometimes it is called an "immigrant" mindset, but it is what most of us know as a growth mindset. And companies who learn how to nourish it reap an even greater reward— leaders who will take them to the next level.

FIVE | THE HOLY GRAIL

"Let me learn as much as I can."

"When war came to my village, we fled to Ethiopia. If we went back, we would be killed."

Werga leans forward in his seat, hands clasped. Six-foot-four with midnight black skin, a rare seriousness replaces the huge smile more commonly displayed on his face.

The year was 1996 when he and his father, brother, wife, and two children were forced to flee. While the world was readying for the Olympic games in Atlanta, his family was walking through the desert with thousands of other displaced Sudanese.

Candidly, he shares, "I had one child on my neck, and one [child] on my back. They would start crying because there was no food and no drink. People were starving. You would see people dying."

But dehydration and malnutrition weren't the only enemies. There were wild animals— lions, hyenas, and crocodiles— also looking for their next meal to eat. Werga was 24 years old, and instead of settling into life, he was starting over. Every dream he ever had for his family and career was abandoned back at his village.

Now, a camp full of makeshift tents was their home. Food was the currency. Letters traced in the dirt were his children's only source of education, *and a ticket elsewhere was their only source of hope.*

"UNHCR would nail a list to a tree, every month or so – a list of everyone [cleared to] go to America, Australia, and other countries," Werga shared. Every month they checked the list, but it would be three years before their names appeared.

As they prepared to leave their familiar surroundings, a mixture of fear and relief flooded Werga. They had survived the treacherous African desert, *but could they survive starting over in an entirely different country?*

. . . .

Before we dive into another attribute of the refugee workforce, let's recap what we've discovered thus far.

First, refugees are legal to work, dependable, and have lower rates of drug usage than native-born Americans. In a day and age of low dependability and high rates of drug test failures, these basic traits alone make refugees a prudent choice to fill our growing labor shortages.

We've also seen how enthusiastic and loyal refugees are within a welcoming work environment. They are not only highly productive, but their gratitude makes them eager to recruit others as well.

Every trait of the refugee workforce we've discussed thus far, has been carefully supported by data and research. However, I would be remiss to not share one more. This final attribute isn't backed by scientific research (yet), but is evident in nearly every encounter my team and I have had with the refugee community over the past five years.

It is a quality every company desires in an employee, but few have come to expect: a growth mindset. But before we articulate the reasons why refugees are more prone to have it, let's define what a growth mindset is, exactly, and take a look at its opposing counterpart.

> **GROWTH MINDSET IS A QUALITY EVERY COMPANY DESIRES IN AN EMPLOYEE, BUT FEW HAVE COME TO EXPECT.**

Growth vs. Fixed Mindset

The first person to develop the theory behind growth and fixed mindsets was psychologist Carol Dweck. She theorized that every individual carries with them a fixed or growth mindset shaping how they interact with the world around them.

A person with a *fixed mindset* believes their level of talent and intelligence is relatively unchangeable. They believe they are limited by the body, brain, and circumstances they were born with (i.e. "I'm just not good at math," "nobody in my family has ever gone to college"). When they find themselves stuck in an undesirable circumstance, they simply accept it. They avoid any situations or challenges that may lead to embarrassment.

Conversely, individuals with a growth mindset believe one's talent, intellect, and condition in life can all be improved with enough hard work and perseverance. *Anything is possible.* This paradigm motivates them to embrace challenges, and take hold of every opportunity to learn new skills and improve themselves.

By these simple explanations, it should be obvious why companies would want their employees to possess the latter mindset. Employees embody the company culture—where the culture goes, so goes the company. Therefore companies comprised of employees who are consistently learning and re-inventing themselves will, likewise, grow and innovate.

When it comes to employees who are eager to learn and grow, few can compare to the zeal of the refugee workforce. Immigrants, as a whole, have long made a name for themselves in the business world for their entrepreneurial spirits and groundbreaking patents. First and second generation immigrants have played a role in founding nearly half of our nation's top one hundred Fortune 500 companies, including Google, Apple, and AT&T.[63]

But is this merely a coincidence, or is there a reason behind their success? This is a question researchers have long been intrigued by, and their conclusions seem to point to the circumstances leading up to, and during, their resettlement.

Planned or unplanned, you have to admit it takes great fortitude to move to an unfamiliar country and start over again. For refugees, the character developed while navigating some of the worst situations imaginable also proves to be beneficial in the long-run.

So what are these growth mindset attributes, how did they develop, and what are their benefits? Let's take a look at a few of them.

Resilience

The first characteristic of refugees, common among those with a growth mindset, is resilience. Over the past several years, our company has conducted nearly one hundred interviews with refugees and the individuals, companies and nonprofits supporting them. If there's one word we hear time and time again describing this exceptional people group it is "resilient."

Resilience is defined as the "**ability to recover readily** from illness, depression, **adversity**, or the like; buoyancy."[64]

By the time they are resettled, refugees have often suffered years, even decades, of hardship, building within them an enormous amount of **inner strength and perseverance**. More than simply enduring life's punches, they have learned to get back up in the face of adversity, time and again.

It's easy to see how beneficial this trait can be within the context of the workplace. While other workers are more likely to quit in the face of failure or difficulty, refugee employees aren't easily deterred. In a healthy culture (we'll get to that shortly), they hardly seem bothered by challenges and setbacks. They simply keep doing what they've always done — *getting back up.*

Recently, a local warehouse hired a group of new arrivals to the U.S. The company committed to pay for their transportation for the first three months, as long as the new employees agreed to engage in ESL classes, obtain their driver's licenses, and purchase a vehicle by the end of those three months. Fikre and Patrick took the challenge, and each failed their drivers test *four times,* but kept trying. On their 90th day of employment, they passed their tests *and* split the cost of a used minivan.

The next day, Fikre and Patrick loaded up their minivan with fellow refugee co-workers and drove to work for the first time. How's that for a growth mindset experiment? In ninety days they navigated a new culture, a new language, and a new job while achieving a level of financial literacy. These two reached a goal most of us would never dare to attempt. Oh, and by the way, they each received a promotion and pay increase on day 91 when they took on a new challenge: learning to drive the company forklift.

Adaptability
A second growth mindset attribute we see in refugees is adaptability. While resilience refers to an individual's ability to bounce back from setbacks, adaptability has to do with their ability to prepare for, and adjust to new and changing conditions.

The refugee workforce is great at adaptation because they know what it's like to have their "normal" taken away, and to be left with no other choice but to adapt. A new country. A new culture. A new career. They must quickly adjust to a new normal, knowing it *could* and most likely *will* change again, in a heartbeat. The result? *They learn to stay on their toes.*

Adaptable employees are a huge asset in the workplace. They are flexible to change, when they know it's good for the long-run. They approach their responsibilities with plans held loosely, knowing those plans may need to adapt in order to succeed. They develop a deep understanding of the fact that *change is necessary to survive.*

. . . .

"When I came to this country, I worked really hard," Werga says as he thinks about what it was like to start over. "I kept working and working, but I didn't see anything that I was working for. I talked to my wife about it. I said, 'You see, I am working, and you're working, but we're not getting anywhere.' I thought there might be something missing."

Despite years of faithful work, he and his family were still barely scraping by. That was when Werga's wife suggested he pursue skills training so he could work his way into a better job.

"I didn't think about going to school [in the first few years after arriving] because I had a family and my concern was I just needed to go to work to provide for them," he explains.

But Werga knew his wife was right: it was time to go back to school.

Just a few short weeks after their conversation, he started classes at a local technical college with the goal of becoming an HVAC technician. With no prior experience in HVAC, he simply decided he would learn it.

"There are things you just have to do. You have to learn. Anything you believe you can do, you can do it. You *will* do it."

Up until this point, Werga had been a farmer (in Sudan), a janitor, and a warehouse worker for a popular retail store. But now, the desire to improve his family's circumstances was greater than any fear about leaving *comfortable* for the *unknown*.

"I thought, *this is not going to be enough,*" Werga shared. *"I need something else."*

At the recommendation of a friend, he reached out to Luke Keller. Luke had recently started a construction trades training program in Clarkston, Georgia.

A problem solver and smart businessman, Luke had taken notice of two problems: one, the growing need for skilled tradesman in the job market, and two, the reality that many refugees were still living in low-income households even years after resettlement.

He launched what has become Tekton Career Training in 2012 to bridge the gap between the two problems. The organization serves the "displaced and disadvantaged" through four construction trades training programs: welding, electrical, carpentry, and pipe-fitting.

When Werga heard about Tekton, he signed up for not just one, but *two* courses— welding and pipefitting— knowing these skills *plus* the HVAC training would provide him with not only greater opportunity, but greater adaptability within the workplace.

Every weekday he drove to the technical school, and every weeknight he trained at Tekton. On weekends "off" he took on many part-time jobs, and even met with his teacher for extra help.

"I was really learning a lot," he remembers, then admits with a wide grin, *"It was hard!"*

The support of his wife and encouragement from his teacher kept him going. The weeks turned quickly into months. Finally, two years after he began, Werga was finally ready to fully re-enter the workplace, armed with an entirely new skill set.

. . . .

Desire to prove themselves
A third growth mindset attribute we have noted is most, if not all, refugees possess a resolute desire to prove themselves.

I believe one of the greatest tragedies of the refugee crisis is that refugees *want* to contribute meaningfully to society, but are often restricted from opportunities.

"Today, over half the world's refugees are in prolonged refugee situations," Alexander Betts and Paul Collier explain in their book, *Refuge: Rethinking Policy in a Changing World.* "For them, the average length of stay is two decades."[65]

Corralled into refugee camps, in host countries, "The default response has been hopeless. Condemning millions of people to wasting their lives, this approach has contrived the rare folly of being both inhumane and expensive."[66]

By the time refugees are resettled, they are *more than ready* to show the world what they can do.

At this point, I should note there is a *significant* difference between the desire to prove oneself and the desire to impress. The majority of the refugees I've met are not interested in making it *appear* as though they have knowledge and skill they don't actually possess. They are solely interested in working hard to prove they are capable of learning and accomplishing anything they set their minds to.

As you can see from the handful of stories in this book, this thirst for achievement is not easily quenched—

For many of the refugees I have met, it is *insatiable.*

Zinah Ghazi, who we met in chapter two, went back to school after already earning her degree in microbiology in order to position herself for better access to the American workforce. She plans to return again, this time to get a PhD from Harvard.

Robe Kumsa, from chapter three, had no prior experience when she stepped foot in Engent's quality assurance center, but they gave her a shot. She picked up so quickly on the training that the company changed their hiring policies to add her to the team.

Daywoe Nimely had grown tired of his family's financial hardships and moved in pursuit of something more. When we placed him at Gates Corporation, he wasn't shy about his ambitions for a permanent position. He took advantage of every opportunity the company gave him to grow, and in six months his dream came true. Now, he's learning and training even more.

Tekton executive director Laura Green shared a congruent observation about the refugees in the training program, "They come in and the mindset is *'let me learn as much as I can, and then go see what I can do with it.'*" [*]

This growth mindset attribute benefits companies in a big way: motivation. The refugee workforce is not motivated simply to show up and make enough money to get by — they are motivated to bring their best to the table every single day.

Willing to take risks and tolerant of uncertainty
Just like Werga and his wife, many resettling refugees are faced with the fear of whether or not they will not just survive, but *succeed* after resettlement. But despite not knowing whether they will land on two feet, they make the leap anyway.

Maybe it's their confidence in their resilience and ability to adapt, but immigrants as a whole don't seem the slightest bit afraid of failure. They are willing to take big risks for the potential of big reward, much like Werga, who left a comfortable job to invest his time in training with the hope of one day gaining a better job.

Laura says she sees this attribute daily in the men and women Tekton trains: "Because of the journey many have taken in getting here, their depth of 'whatever it takes' is much more profound than others," she shares.

---

[*] Visit **www.refugeeworkforce.com** for our interview with Luke Keller and Laura Green of Tekton Career Training.

"They're willing to sacrifice a *ton*."

Along with their "whatever it takes" grit lies an incredibly high tolerance to the uncertainty associated with risk. Refugees, as a whole, seem better suited to withstand the anxiety associated with change.[67] Maybe it's because, after years of uncertainty, they've learned to be content not knowing all of the answers for tomorrow, while still making the most of today.

But, outside of entrepreneurship, is this attribute good for businesses? The experts agree– yes, it is.

Employees who are risk-takers are more creative, and go on to achieve more than their timid counterparts. Companies don't have to motivate these individuals to innovate, as their minds are already constantly analyzing data and dreaming of new and more efficient ways to do business.

. . . .

Werga had taken a great risk, and put in the work. He had *three certificates* to prove it. Now, he waited to see if it would pay off.

Luke Keller, now President of Amplio Recruiting, placed Werga with a local heating and air company in an entry-level role, shortly after graduation.

Even after two years of extensive training, his job was simply to deliver parts to technicians on site. Werga made the most of the opportunity to learn from other technicians.

For a year, he observed their work and asked questions to gain a better grasp on technique. Next, he moved up to technician *assistant*. In all of his waiting, Werga did not despair. He kept learning and growing, and making the most of every opportunity.

Finally, after years of pursuing every ounce of information he could lay hold of, *he* earned the position of technician. He drives his own company truck, and makes more than triple his former, hourly employee salary— plus benefits.

Even then, he was not satisfied to simply show up and do the work.

Now he's the one helping other soon-to-be technicians.

"If I have all of this knowledge, why should I not give it to other people?" Werga poses the question, rhetorically.

He plans to not only grow with his company, but eventually return to Tekton to help train others in his former situation. "If you just learn something for yourself, it doesn't benefit the rest of the world, it's not going to develop my community" he explains, passionately.

"I want everyone to benefit from me. We are here in this world as tourists. What God has given to me to use, why should I just keep it to myself?"

· · · · · · · · ·

Eager to help others

The final growth mindset attribute we've noted among refugees is their enthusiasm to help others.

This is prevalent within the refugee community as these individuals consistently seem to take what they have been given, what they have learned, and what they have earned, and pay it forward to others. To them, success isn't success until they have benefited others as well.

> SUCCESS ISN'T SUCCESS UNTIL THEY HAVE BENEFITED OTHERS AS WELL.

Unlike the societies in much of the Western world where the focus is on the individual, most refugees come from collective cultures where community is key to strength and survival. Individuals who see life through this paradigm are more "we focused," instead of "me focused," which certainly makes for stronger communities as well as better businesses. Growth mindset employees care not only about their own well-being, but the health and success of the entire company.

For businesses who hire and invest in these individuals, the buck doesn't stop there. These individuals possess a strong sense of responsibility, *and joy,* in sharing their newfound knowledge with anyone who may benefit. And their commitment to invest in others makes them phenomenal leaders at every stage along their career journey.

Nourish vs. Neglect
Resilience, adaptability, desire to prove oneself, a willingness to take risks, and an eagerness to help others are a handful of benefits to hiring employees who have a growth mindset.

At this point, it's important to distinguish that just because an individual possesses these positive qualities doesn't mean the companies who hire them will *automatically* reap the benefits. As in the give-and-take cycle described in chapter four, employers must play their part in encouraging this mindset, lest they squelch it.

Without a nurturing environment, growth mindset employees will become bored and dissatisfied, or feel they are taken for granted. It won't be long before they move on to another company that will support their desire to grow and appreciate their efforts. Conversely, companies that value this mindset and provide healthy paths and boundaries for learning, innovation, and growth will reap loyal employees who stick around for the long-run.

So how can a company be sure it is cultivating an environment encouraging their employees' growth mindset? Let's explore five definitive behaviors growth mindset companies cultivate, and their benefits.

Behavior #1: Growth mindset companies praise right actions. Every employee wants to be recognized for their contributions. As it turns out, most individuals aren't satisfied solely by a paycheck, but have an innate need for verbal affirmation.

The problem is most leaders only praise right results, not right actions. In these environments, only the smartest and most high-achieving workers are recognized. This can become incredibly frustrating to employees who show up every day and put in their best effort, but don't always experience the results they are after. When hitting goals becomes the only aim, employees often either a.) become unmotivated, or b.) do anything (i.e. lie, cheat, and steal) to win. Neither is a desirable outcome.

By encouraging the right actions over right results, you will create a culture where all employees feel appreciated and empowered. This kind of environment is especially important for refugees, most of whom grew up in honor-shame cultures and would rather quit than be publicly embarrassed and shame his or herself.

When you praise right actions, you encourage the behavior and confidence that will sustainably yield the results you're after.

Behavior #2: Growth mindset companies encourage continuous learning. Individuals with a growth mindset recognize their current level of intelligence and experience doesn't have to remain permanent. They are hungry to take in every ounce of information and training they can get their hands on to help them improve.

Companies providing opportunities for these employees to learn by way of books, hands-on training, mentorship, conferences, and more will satisfy this hunger—and see employee commitment spike.

When we started working with Booster Spirit Wear to place refugees in their screen-printing warehouse, they immediately recognized their new employees' insatiable desire to learn. They made a bold decision they felt would best utilize this growth mindset.

They told our employees they were starting in an entry-level position, and would be expected to work a daily eight hour shift, minimum. However, if there was any equipment they wanted to learn how to use, in order to move into a higher-paying position, they could stay after their shift and be paid to train on the equipment.

Each employee would be responsible for finding a mentor, who would also be paid for their time. It was a big risk, but the company knew it would pave the way for a better trained team in the future. James, one of the first employees hired under this program, learned how to operate *every single machine*—and is still with the company four years later.

Behavior #3: Growth mindset companies create and communicate clear career paths. Growth mindset employees left to figure out a career path on their own will usually find one— right out of the company.

> **GROWTH MINDSET EMPLOYEES LEFT TO FIGURE OUT A CAREER PATH ON THEIR OWN WILL USUALLY FIND ONE— RIGHT OUT OF THE COMPANY.**

Commitment is the "holy grail" of what most companies are looking for these days. Every employee represents an investment of time, energy and resources. Employers who want to make the most on this investment need to create *and communicate* a clear and actionable path forward.

If you want good employees to stay, be sure to cast a clear vision for their future within the company. Taking time to do this will create strong loyalty.

Refugees are naturally loyal, where they are welcomed. When given a clear career path, they are not only more loyal, but sprint harder and faster than anyone else I've ever witnessed.

We recently began working with RockTech in Detroit, Michigan. They design, manufacture and install structural support for factories, and need welders, pipe-fitters, and electricians to do so. They've committed to hire and train refugees with no prior construction experience. The employees will be paid a living wage while they learn valuable skills as apprentices.

RockTech has even identified a path for entry level hires to earn promotions as they developed their skills. This is certainly an upfront sacrifice of both time and money, but will have a tremendous long-term impact for everyone involved.

Behavior #4: Growth mindset companies provide actionable, constructive feedback. The difference between criticism and feedback is investment.

While criticism is centered on finding fault, feedback communicates both an honest review *and* corrective solutions. Criticism squelches the confidence needed to get back up and keep going. Growth mindset employees thrive when they are given the information and tools they need to learn from their mistakes, and improve next time.

A refugee's desire to prove his or herself makes them eager to please every time. They would rather hear honest feedback, even when it hurts, rather than find out later you were disappointed in their performance. When giving feedback, it's important to remember this: you can still be accepting of a person, while expressing disapproval of their actions.

Behavior #5: Growth mindset companies are accepting of failure and risk. One final consideration, for companies who desire to nourish a growth mindset, is this: create an environment where employees have the freedom to take smart risks.

Failure must be acceptable. Smart leaders know failure is not an end, rather a stepping stone on the journey to success.

Growth mindset employees are inherently willing to take smart risks. When a company nurtures an accepting environment, it frees these employees up to be more innovative.

Innovation isn't just about creating new products, ideas or methods, but improving upon the old ones. When we first placed several refugees at Compac Industries, a leading baby product manufacturer in Atlanta, one of them suggested inventory be moved to shelves right next to their work stations, instead of where it had always been— on the other side of the warehouse. No one had ever considered this detail before, but this one, simple action resulted in an immediate and drastic boost in productivity.

Nurturing an environment that is accepting of failure and risk will ensure your company won't get stuck in the rut of "this is the way it's always been done," by encouraging constant innovation.

Speaking of innovation, hiring refugees with a growth mindset is not the only way to expand innovation at your company. Unbelievably, there is yet another way hiring refugees contribute to company growth.

Diverse teams, made up of varying perspectives, skills, and experiences, will produce the innovation most companies are after simply because different ideas do not develop naturally out of similar minds.

Diversity in the workplace is more than just ethically sound, these days— it's becoming highly sought after. In our next chapter, we'll dive into this additional bonus of hiring the refugee workforce.

SIX | DEEP & WIDE DIVERSITY

"I think we owe a lot of our success to our diversity."

When Dick James was approached with the opportunity to purchase a dilapidated apartment complex in East Atlanta, he had no idea how life-changing the deal would be.

In 2006, R James Properties was already managing 1,500 units across Atlanta. The property in consideration was located in a little-known town named Clarkston. It was unkempt, and needed significant renovations. And yet something within him compelled the industrious entrepreneur to say "yes" to the challenge.

Dick placed his son, Kelly James, in charge of the new location, hoping he could turn things around at the failing property. Together they began the hard work of restoring the 213 units and filling them with residents.

It wasn't long before Kelly recognized there was something very different about the Clarkston community. Every day on the job seemed like a stroll through Epcot at Disney.

A family from Burma,
A couple from Congo,
Six siblings from Syria,
And an elderly woman from Somalia...

A kaleidoscope of ethnicities cohabitated within every building. He had stumbled upon the refugee community.

Kelly knew very little about refugees, but over the next several months he came to one key conclusion: *they were terrific residents.*

The only individuals he had to evict at Clarkston Townhomes, thus far, were Americans. Meanwhile, his refugee residents maintained a $0 balance, *consistently*, at the end of every month— a phenomena that wasn't taking place even at the company's class A apartments. Not only were they paying their rent without fail, these individuals were incredibly thankful. Their gratitude was conveyed not just by mouth, but in action, as they conscientiously followed the property rules. Both the residents and the company were happy, and before long, the property attained a rare 100% occupancy.

Kelly recognized the incredible potential, and turned his focus on keeping and attracting more of these excellent renters. Unfortunately, his ability to speak only English and Spanish left much lost in translation. He struggled both to understand his residents' problems, and to communicate expectations. Kelly sought the help of refugee non-profit organizations to translate several of the company's pamphlets. Eventually the frustrated leader came to a clear revelation: to effectively reach his diverse consumer base, he would need an equally diverse team of employees to serve them.

He placed a call to New American Pathways, a nearby refugee nonprofit. Paedia Mixon answered the phone, hearing Kelly's eager voice asking, "What language do most refugees speak?" The wise executive director returned a few questions, finally concluding that Arabic would be most helpful.

"Great!" Kelly responded, "Can you send me someone who can speak both Arabic and English as soon as possible?"

. . . .

Diversity is a popular topic of conversation these days, especially in the workplace. Current studies confirm the building of a diverse team is not only ethical, but comes with a broad range of benefits. Research has established what many have suspected for years— and others just stumbled upon by accident— diverse teams are happier, more creative, and better performing than those that are homogenous.

A simple Google search will produce a plethora of blogs on "How to Increase Workplace Diversity," or "4 Smart Ways to Make Your Company More Diverse." Interviews with global companies like IKEA and AT&T attribute much of their success to diversity, which has prompted many to attempt to emulate them. A 2018 study by LinkedIn reported more than three out of every four U.S. companies are making diversity a primary focus.[68] Unfortunately, many are going about it wrong. Without the right parameters in place, diversity can be more harmful than it is effective.

For the fullest benefits of diversity to manifest, I've found there are some caveats. So before we dive into *even more* benefits of hiring the refugee workforce, let me take a few moments to lay a little groundwork.

Deep and wide
First, authentic diversity is not achieved simply by sprinkling a few minority individuals onto a team. I've known many companies taking this approach, setting out just to check a few boxes on paper. This surface-level "diversity," is incredibly ineffective.

True diversity runs deep and wide. In an authentically diverse company, employees represent a broad span of age, gender, religion, ethnicity, and background.

But not only should diversity spread wide, it runs deep—throughout every level. In a survey by Glassdoor, 41% of employees felt their executive team was not diverse.[69] True diversity is not relegated to the few bottom rungs, but offers equal opportunity at every level based on merit, *regardless of age, gender, or ethnicity.*

Diversity should be an ongoing posture of openness, instead of a *percentage* to be obtained. That brings me to point number two: diversity, in and of itself, cannot be effective alone.

Diversity, *plus*

You may recall in chapter four we looked at how the act of hiring refugees alone won't guarantee success, but must be paired with *integration*. Then, in chapter five we recognized the fact that companies won't reap the benefits of employees with a growth mindset without nourishing it.

Likewise, diversity, too, requires a "partner." So before you begin attempting to stack a team of people who look and think differently together, know this: *inclusion* must be the forerunner.

Inclusion is defined as "the act of including." In inclusive work environments, *every* employee's voice matters. Participation is not limited to a primary race or gender. *Everyone is a valuable player in the game.*

Not only that, but every employee is comfortable bringing their whole self— their values, beliefs, ideas, and perspectives— to the table. There is no fear of alienation; there are no outsiders. Everyone belongs.

> **DISCRIMINATION AND DIVERSITY CANNOT COEXIST.**

Inclusion, like integration, does not happen by accident. It takes intention. It must be upheld by leadership as a fundamental standard, and ingrained within company culture. Discrimination and diversity cannot coexist. Any bigotry must be shut down immediately.

Inclusion also requires an acknowledgment and acceptance of the hard work it will take to not only press on through the initial challenges, but also set aside one's personal preference and biases.

Ignoring diversity, and the resulting challenges, doesn't work. Rather, you acknowledge and accept the obstacles involved, set your sights on the goal, and remain committed to see things through to the worthwhile end.

"Diversity has to be a conscious effort," says Betty Ng, CEO of Inspiring Diversity, "and companies wanting to recruit and retain diverse employees need to create a culture of inclusion, which needs to start at the top and needs to be woven into day-to-day operations."[70]

At Amplio, our clients are always coming up with fantastic ways to become more inclusive within their diverse workplace. One of my favorite examples is Tendon Systems, a company manufacturing post-tensioning systems and barrier cables for advanced concrete construction. CEO Brad Reffensprerger is also the Georgia Secretary of State and has seen the tremendous impact of the refugee workforce first-hand at his company. We've placed nearly 25 Congolese men at Tendon and their hard work has resulted in a surge in production at their Atlanta plant.

As the team at Tendon began to embrace their new co-workers, they did something we've seen very few companies do in order to pursue inclusivity. Instead of the typical knee-jerk reaction to communication challenges, which is to move employees into English language courses, their team took it one step further. With inclusion as the goal, the supervisors decided first to learn some conversational French to communicate better with their new, dependable employees. The story of the refugee workforce is still being written at Tendon, but no doubt it will be a long and prosperous relationship for both parties because of their wise and empathetic leadership.

Workplaces that are exclusive, whether knowingly or not, block some of the most talented, innovative, and insightful employees from ever entering. Unless you are incredibly meticulous, it's not always easy to recognize areas of weakness when it comes to company inclusivity. That is why it is important to solicit honest feedback on a frequent basis, from both an outside perspective, and from your minority employees.

As you become more inclusive, you will find your labor pool begin to widen. Similar to measuring right actions instead of right results from our last chapter, focusing on inclusive actions will move you closer to having diverse teams producing great results. To move the needle on diversity at your company, however, our third and final caveat is vital.

Focus on the right people
When our team began interviewing our clients to gain more insight in regards to diversity, a common theme emerged. **Some of the most successful diverse companies admitted diversity was never the goal, but rather became a byproduct of building an effective team**. It wasn't that they were against diversity. Rather they created an inclusive environment, and sought *the right people*, regardless of age, ethnicity, gender or background.

Kelly James, from our opening story in this chapter, began to think outside the box when it came to hiring in order to keep his renters happy. Now he runs one of the most diverse and inclusive companies we've ever had the privilege of serving.

He shared, "While we are a very diverse company, we actually have not worked to cultivate diversity. **On the contrary, we work to find and place individuals in positions where they are most likely to succeed, regardless of any arbitrary characteristics such as ethnicity, gender, etc.** The diversity of our team has been the result of years of cultivating a great team of employees."

Diversity in the workforce, is not only beautiful, it's productive, when companies first:

- Understand what true diversity means
- Create structures to support it
- Cultivate an inclusive work environment, and
- Focus on hiring the right people

You may be thinking *Chris that seems like a lot of work.*

And, quite honestly, *yes it is*— until you consider the dividends resulting from the investment.

Over the years, I've seen many companies hanging on by a thread make a complete turnaround after committing to inclusivity and filling positions with the refugee workforce. But the cherry on top, was the diverse culture. Boosted productivity and a better bottom line are great in the short-term— but to sustain success over the long haul you'll need a diverse culture. Let's unpack the benefits of diversity that make that type of long-term success possible.

. . . .

The next morning Kelly James found himself sitting across the table from Kareem, a clean-cut, long-faced former General in the Iraqi Air Force.

He spoke fluent Arabic and English, which met Kelly's most pressing need of someone who could communicate to residents. He also figured that a man who previously commanded a military could certainly handle a few mild-mannered residents. Kelly hired Kareem on the spot.

"I never questioned whether he could do the job because he wasn't an American." Kelly remembers. "I've come across that kind of attitude before, and I quickly let those team members know we don't tolerate that."

Kareem quickly proved himself as a valuable asset. Communication with residents improved, and business was generally running more smoothly. It wasn't long before he began moving up in the company.

Kelly later found out Al Qaeda had blown-up Kareem's house, killed his twin brother, and shot Kareem down *twice* in combat. One of those times, he survived by floating in the Persian Gulf for *three days.*

His determined spirit often came in handy, but especially one unforgettable week in 2009 when it rained for seven days straight.

A blurry-eyed Kelly awakened at 4am to a knock at the door, and Kareem on the other side with some bad news: fifty units were flooded with more than a foot of water. Kelly and Kareem immediately went to work. They spent 18-hour days together for *the next week* to repair the damage, neither backing down, and both doing whatever it took to keep residents happy.

"Kareem has a military mindset. You give him a mission, he takes the hill," Kelly shared. After such great success at their first Clarkston property, they bought another in 2009, then a third in 2011. As their properties grew, so did their team—both in numbers, *and in diversity.*

Mustafa, a former computer tech, took over managing Clarkston Townhomes. Before coming to the U.S. as a refugee, he traveled with his wife and four kids through the mountains of Iraq to escape death.

Amer ran a textbook company supplying Syria's schools with books before the war. Now he's a manager at Sage Point Apartments, the newest R James owned property.

Karimi helped the U.S. military in his home country of Afghanistan. He moved to the U.S. after his life was threatened by the Taliban. Now he is one of the company's best maintenance technicians.[*]

The R James team has grown to an impressive 115 full-time, "high-caliber" individuals, as Kelly calls them, some from right here in Georgia, and others from around the world.

A couple dozen are former refugees, who hold positions at every level of leadership, from leasing agents to maintenance technicians. R James Properties didn't hire them to earn a tax credit, or an award for being the best place to work. They became a diverse workforce out of necessity, but quickly realized "treating people the way you want to be treated" is a great way to build a strong culture.

---

[*] Visit **www.refugeeworkforce.com** to watch an interview with Karimi.

. . . .

Access to a wider range of skills and talent
Perhaps the most obvious benefit of diversity is access to an equally diverse set of skills and talent on your team.

"Different people have different strengths, and are able to bring to the table different life experiences," advises Kelly James. A broad spectrum of experience and ability will curb blind spots and talent gaps on your team.

And because of their growth mindset, refugees and immigrants close that gap even further. Remember: what they don't know how to do, they'll learn. Kelly shared a great example:

"Two years ago we supervised a big rehab at a rough complex in Atlanta that had been mismanaged for a decade. We had to replace everything— sinks, countertops, etcetera— to make them rent-ready. We hired a bunch of guys from Amplio, and they blew through those units. One of them suggested we could save time and money by resurfacing the countertops instead. We showed them a YouTube video, and they learned how to do it. They were so willing to tackle the project, and be enthusiastic about it."

Diversity increases a team's capacity to not only complete the tasks at hand, but develop new, more effective methods. We'll cover that in our next benefit.

Increased innovation + creativity
If you'll remember, we ended our last chapter talking about innovation. Creativity and innovation are often used interchangeably, but are distinctly different. While innovating is developing a new approach to an old method, creating insinuates making something altogether new. However *both* are side benefits to a diverse workplace.

A study by *Economic Geography* confirmed "increased cultural diversity is a boon to **innovativeness.**" The same report revealed "businesses run by culturally diverse leadership teams were more likely to develop **new** products...."[71]

This noticeable advantage is largely attributed to employees' multicultural experiences, which causes them to approach life from more than a single, limited perspective. As Kelly James put it, simply, "Different life experiences result in different ways of approaching problems."

When different points of view converge, they often result in a highly-coveted "Aha" moment. A new approach is born, a new idea, a new product.

Karina Rosas, team leader at a local cosmetic manufacturer working with us to provide jobs for hundreds of refugees, shared, "When you have employees from different countries and backgrounds, you not only have different talents, but different ways of thinking. We listen to their ideas. In the end, it is a good product."

Sometimes that "good product" is *better customer service*. Because, along with this broadened perspective comes greater insight into the consumers' needs and wants.

Greater insight
When Kelly James recognized units were quickly filling with customers that didn't look like, act like, or talk like him, he knew he needed to hire someone that could bridge the language gap, and better help him understand their needs.

By bringing Kareem and other diverse individuals to his team, Kelly was better able to discern the best way to market to, communicate with, and serve individuals in the diverse community.

A company that restores homes after fire and water damage recently hired a few of our guys. Najib, an Afghani carpenter was one of them. He began rebuilding dressers, chairs, and tables to match their pre-disaster condition. On many occasions, the company would be asked to restore pieces of wood furniture with ornate carvings throughout.

The owner had all but given up on finding anyone who could accomplish such detailed work. He figured it was a lost skill – that is until Najib proved him wrong.

The talented carpenter took one look at an old family photo of an heirloom dresser, and set off to work. A few days later the dresser which was once damaged to the point of no return was fully restored to its former glory.

Before, the company didn't know such a great need for the talent existed. Now, they're winning contracts based solely on providing the service.[*]

Broadened perspective leads to greater insight, which then lends itself to another benefit of a diverse workforce: better decision making.

Better decision making

Every company wants their employees to make better decisions. Improved decision making, in the end, drives better company performance.

In a somewhat surprising study, the "decision-making database," Cloverpop, measured and compared the decisions of 200 different businesses. Their conclusion was this: "as the diversity of teams increases so does the chance of making better decisions. In fact, the most diverse teams made better decisions 87% of the time."[72]

Eighty-seven percent. *That's astounding.*

---

[*] Visit **www.refugeeworkforce.com** for an interview with Najib about his work, and meaningful display of gratitude to former President George W. Bush.

But companies who put a high price on time (don't we all?) might find their second discovery even more interesting: they make those decisions up to two times faster, in half the number of meetings.[73]

I'll take faster decisions in half the meetings! How about you??

At this point let me refer back to my second caveat: it all boils down to how inclusively those diverse teams function. "Inclusive decision making is not just about having diverse perspectives present in a team," Cloverpop reiterates. *"It's about whether the decision-making process actively incorporates those views."*

But before you start calculating how much time you could save if half the meetings on your calendar were unnecessary due to the efficiency of a diverse culture, just wait. There's *more.*

. . . .

Kelly's not shy about his goal of "apartments so clean your mama would move in it," and that level of excellence has certainly set R James Properties apart from the competition. Another distinguishing trait is the company's low rate of turnover. Not just among its residents, but among the employees who work there.

At a time when most companies can hardly find or keep dependable workers, very few members of Kelly's team venture out in pursuit of something else. And the few that do, he says, often return. As it turns out, everyone wins when you treat people right and provide good service.

Kelly gets a lot of invites these days— to everything from dinner parties to gym meet ups. His employees don't just work together, they live life together.

They are more than coworkers. They are family.

Never could he have imagined a team so diverse, but neither could he have dreamed of being this successful. R James Properties now manages more than 4,000 units across the Atlanta area, and has been named in Atlanta Business Chronicle's "Top 25 Apartment Management Companies" multiple years. Kelly has high hopes of continuing to grow and expand.

"I think we owe a lot of our success to our diversity," Kelly shares, "Employees from a wide variety of backgrounds will often come up with new ways of approaching challenges. But rather than working to impose diversity, we have focused on treating our employees fairly, while helping them to achieve shared goals. Diversity has followed."[*]

. . . .

Increased Morale + Employee Engagement
As the fight to hold onto good workers continues to intensify, more companies are taking a closer look at their morale.

Morale correlates to the level of satisfaction employees feel toward their place of work. Perhaps one of the greatest shifts since the Baby Boomer generation entered the workforce is that modern-day employees are more concerned with gaining *meaning*, not just *money*, from their work. A happy, healthy work environment matters. When morale becomes low, most workers will simply go somewhere else.

Companies with high morale are associated with high trust, low absenteeism, greater collaboration, and less accidents. When these attributes are present, the result is employees who not only stay, but *stay engaged.*

High morale is another common characteristic of the diverse workplace.

---

[*] Visit our resource page at **www.refugeeworkforce.com** for a video interview with Kelly James

In companies where inclusivity is upheld and every voice matters, employees know they are not only heard, but valued. The result of this mutually respectful environment is natural engagement, and higher levels of performance overall.

As in the case of R James Properties, relational engagement takes place not only inside, but outside of work as well. Despite what the news may portray, people love to engage with individuals who are different. *What fun would it be to live in a world where everyone was just like us?*

Albritha Booker, was a refugee from Liberia and now proudly can call herself a U.S. citizen. She is going on two years in her role at the cosmetic manufacturing company mentioned earlier. She told us, "My favorite part about my job is the diversity. I love my job. I like being with people from different nationalities."

> "RATHER THAN WORKING TO IMPOSE DIVERSITY, WE HAVE FOCUSED ON TREATING OUR EMPLOYEES FAIRLY, WHILE HELPING THEM TO ACHIEVE SHARED GOALS. DIVERSITY HAS FOLLOWED."

Many of our clients communicate to us the positive impact diversity has had on their entire team.

Gourmet Foods supervisor, Orlando Morrow, shared, "I've got a melting pot on my shift. Iraqis, Congolese, Angola, Eritreans, Latinas, Syrians, Caucasians— all these different people mixing together, and they're all friends. It's great to see. They work together, eat together, even do outside social functions together. They're mixing inside and outside of work, and learning each other's cultures."

While I can't promise endless potluck invitations, I can say with confidence a harmonious workplace will result in keeping employees around.

Better recruitment

In case you forgot, here's a reminder: Employees who are happy at work are obviously more likely to tell others, and higher recruitment is the outcome. This is especially true within the refugee community as these individuals are eager to help one another out.

I mentioned earlier that modern-day job seekers aren't content to settle for just good money anymore. Diversity isn't just appealing to refugees, and other minority groups, but most job seekers. "An organization known for its fair employment practices and appreciation for diverse talent is better able to attract a wider pool of qualified applicants," shared Betty Ng, Inspiring Diversity CEO.[74]

A report by Glassdoor on diversity in the workplace showed, "**67 percent of active and passive job seekers said a diverse workforce is an important factor when evaluating companies and job offers.**"[75] This stat shines hope on the future of equity in the workplace.

In consideration of the shift from "employees contending for jobs", to "jobs contending for employees", companies must take their values into consideration in order to remain competitive. This brings us to the next-to-last benefit on our list.

Better reputation

Everyone in business understands that reputation matters. This is why company leaders work so hard to build and protect theirs.

When it comes to diversity, inclusive workplaces lead to better decisions and higher morale, which leads to happier employees, and an overall better reputation.

This has played out favorably for Technocycle, an IT recycling warehouse in Houston, Texas. One of the first things Kamengu, a Congolese refugee remarked to us about the job was the moral character and strong values represented by the company's leadership. He loves telling others from his community about the company values which has created a waiting list of applicants for warehouse positions.

Something else to consider concerning reputation, is that the up-and-coming Generation Z is on track to become "the most influential generation in America to date,"[76] with earnings already estimated at $153 billion. With this in mind, it's important to note their feelings toward brands. Surveys of this group show they are less trusting than previous generations and "want to see authenticity in marketing, including proof and a culture to back up claims of strong company values."[77]

As the debate surrounding immigration heightens and becomes more polarized, many companies are left to wonder how their outward stance toward refugees, in particular, might impact their reputation.

If this is you, then I have some good news. A study conducted by the NYU Stern School of Business shows "brands can consider making commitments to support refugees, knowing that, on net, U.S. consumers support these actions and are more likely to purchase from brands that make them." Their findings, derived from studying a diverse group of 7,139 consumers from across the U.S., revealed nearly half were more likely to purchase a brand if they knew the company was committed to refugee support. And consumers under the age of 35 were upwards of 60% more likely.[78]

Greater talent.
Expanded insight.
Better decision making.
Higher morale.
Improved recruitment.
And an overall better reputation.

All these things come together to produce our final, and most notable benefit:

Sustainable performance + profit
This is it. The result every company is after—consistent performance leading to predictable profit over the long haul.

This is the pot of gold at the end of the rainbow driving the majority of business decisions. This is the reason why many companies, as I mentioned earlier, set out to cultivate a diverse workforce in the first place. And it's true, leaders who are wise enough to prepare the "soil" with inclusive practices will, in the end, reap a great harvest of sustainable performance and profit.

How much better? Upwards of 35%, according to *McKinsey & Company's* 2015 "Diversity Matters" report.[79]

"Companies in the top quartile for racial/ethnic diversity were 35 percent more likely to have financial returns above their national industry median," the report explains. "The reverse is also true, companies in the bottom quartile in both gender and ethnicity underperformed the other three quartiles."[80]

Obviously the better decision making, higher morale, and improved recruitment comes into play. But remember our second caveat, diversity *plus* inclusion? McKinsey's conclusion agrees:

"This correlation does not prove that the relationship is causal—that greater gender and ethnic diversity in corporate leadership automatically translates into more profit…" the report adds. "But rather indicates that **companies that commit to diverse leadership are more successful.**"[81]

While diversity cannot be the sole reason for hiring the refugee workforce, it is, most certainly, an advantageous result. Cultivate an inclusive environment, focus on hiring the right people, and treat your employees well. Workers who are happy, valued, and belong will benefit your company greatly in the long-run.

Who benefits the most?
At this point, we've spent the past four chapters walking through the benefits of the refugee workforce to companies. In the next chapter we'll look at what refugees are getting out of all of this.

Outside of a paycheck, what do *they* gain from showing up and giving 110%, day after day?

The short answer is: more than you may think.

For refugees, establishing employment is *foundational* to rebuilding their lives after resettlement. In our next few pages, we'll look at why welcoming them into the American workplace is the single most impactful way we can help them.

SEVEN | FLOURISHING

"A good job is peace of mind."

"It was night. If they found anyone from my village they were going to shoot them. We fled. We left everything."

Ziwati's soft voice translates her older sister's story into English.

It's been twenty years since her family ran from the rebels, tearing through Congo with their unrelenting army, but Amnobe Pilipili still remembers the incident like it was yesterday.

Her family endured an arduous three-day walk to the north, where life would be "a little safer," but when it came to war, no area of Congo was exempt. So Amnobe's dad used the little money they had to pay for a boat ride across Lake Tanganyika to the Nyarugusu refugee camp in Tanzania.

"It was sad," Amnobe shares in broken English. "To leave home is no good. Cry all the time."

Life in the camp was hard. It was overfilled and under-resourced. Families struggled to meet their basic needs. The local "school" was sub-par, and didn't even teach English. Instead, Amnobe spent her time helping her dad sell goods. He visited neighboring cities to purchase shoes, which she would then sell to other refugees within the camp.

Her family spent seven long years in Nyarugusu. Eventually, Amnobe fell in love and married. Shortly thereafter, they were delighted when she gave birth to a son.

Her husband, also a Congo native, longed to return to his home village, and Amnobe agreed to follow. They returned to their beloved country, but tragedy struck again. Only this time, it would be more devastating than the last.

Amnobe wipes the tears falling from her eyes as she describes, in French, what happened next. As they fled for their lives a second time, her son became lost in the chaotic crowd. Despite desperate searching, they never found him.

Today, he would be eleven.

. . . .

While there is a lot of substantial evidence to be found concerning the value of refugees to companies, there has been far less research conducted on the benefits of employment for refugees.

In this chapter, I'll be speaking largely from observation and experience on this subject.

Every day, resettled individuals from the Middle East, Southeast Asia, South America, and all over Africa step into our Amplio offices looking for work. We have the honor and joy to walk these individuals through the process of applying for what is often their first job in the U.S., and a front-row seat to the transformative nature of work, in particular within the context of the refugee experience.

Amnobe came to us for help near the end of 2017. She spoke only broken English, and brought one of her eight sisters with her to translate.

After losing her son, her family spent several more years living displaced in Kenya, while waiting on approval for resettlement. Finally, Amnobe stepped onto an airplane for the very first time, and when she stepped off began her new life in the United States.

Resettlement had not been easy for her and her growing family. After coming to Clarkston, Amnobe, like many refugees, had taken the first job she could find - at a local chicken factory. She worked the eight-hour night shift, commuting in a packed van for an hour each way.

Eventually she transferred to a slightly better job, but as a mom of two young children, juggling the long hours with responsibilities at home were hardly worth the menial pay.

After years of insecurity, she wanted a stable home— *a stable life*— and in order to do that, she knew she first needed stable employment.

Roots + Security
The first and perhaps most underrated benefit of employment to refugees is the ability to establish strong roots, and regain a sense of security.

One of our most beloved team members in our Atlanta office, Bethelhem, resettled in Clarkston from Ethiopia. As a recruiter for us, she helps job applicants get through the application and placement process. Betty, as we call her, speaks French, Amharic and English fluently, all with a beautiful smile, making her the most popular staff member in the community. She told us, "I had a friend who gave [my husband and me] a bedroom to stay in when we came. But I felt insecure because I didn't have a job. Nothing was consistent. I didn't know what was going to come tomorrow. I thought, *I have to find a job so I can start my life.*"

In that candid statement, Betty gave voice to the unspoken cry of many refugees when they enter our office— they are weary not so much from the loss they've endured, but from the resulting instability.

> **"I THOUGHT, I HAVE TO FIND A JOB SO I CAN START MY LIFE."**

One day these individuals were just going about their business, and the next day, life as they knew it, was over. Nothing was familiar. Nothing was guaranteed. Every day, every moment, became a gamble for them.

Resettlement, contrary to what one might think, is not an automatic end to this struggle. It is the beginning to that end. Now, there is the tedious task of rebuilding. Security is more than reliable income or money in the bank— it is familiar, safe surroundings, friends you can count on, and a consistent place to lay down your head at the end of the day.

Before any refugee can rebuild his or her life, and begin to dream again, it is essential that they establish roots. And establishing themselves in the American workplace is often one of the first.

When Amnobe came to us, we were able to place her in a job at a cosmetics manufacturer providing living wage pay and predictable hours just minutes from her home. Many of her coworkers were refugees just like her. All of them describe the work environment as "more like family."

When we interviewed Amnobe, just a couple months after starting her new job, she no longer seemed desperate or fearful. Though she and the company were still trying to determine her "sweet spot," she seemed settled, confident, and hopeful for her future.

> **SHE WAS HANDED THE KEYS TO HER FIRST PERMANENT HOME IN OVER TWENTY YEARS.**

Those roots were now a foundation on which she could build on. It wasn't long before her eyes were set on her next goal: saving enough money for a down payment on a house. Our second benefit of stable employment is what enabled her to do just that.

Financial Health

The most obvious advantage of having a job (and probably the first benefit that popped into your head when we started this chapter) is income.

Income serves as a vehicle to move refugees back to a state of self-sufficiency. Do not underestimate the power of independence. Without a living wage job, any individual will remain in a perpetual state of relying on others for their needs. I've never met a refugee who wants to live like that.

Refugees need access to some public benefits when they arrive nearly empty-handed. In chapter two, we covered the basic financial assistance refugees receive upon arrival, and demonstrated how the long term fiscal benefits far exceeds the short term costs. There are, of course, a plethora of other programs and organizations existing solely to ensure refugees have access to necessities while they gain their footing.

I've said it before but it's worth repeating— nearly every refugee I've met, while grateful for these services, desires *opportunity* more than anything.

As the Tent Partnership for Refugees succinctly states in its report on how to quickly get refugees into work, "As well as being good for society, working benefits refugees themselves. While they have suffered immensely, they typically do not want to be treated as victims or charity cases. They want to start rebuilding their lives and become self-reliant again."[82]

This reminds me of the old saying, "If you give a man a fish, you feed him for a day. But if you teach a man to fish, you feed him for a lifetime." Refugees aren't looking for free fish. They are happy to earn them. And when they do, they are wise about leveraging those "fish" for a better life for themselves and their families.

I'm often shocked by their ability to achieve their personal and financial goals. But I'm not the only one. Cody Lagana, a team leader at Storr Office Environments, in Raleigh, told us, "It's crazy to me that I have contractors I've worked with for the past two years that haven't been able to save up for a car, yet our refugee employees are doing that almost immediately."

Personal transportation is often a refugee's first major investment. While they'll do anything to get to work— walk, bike, carpool, and take public transportation— owning their own vehicle can be life-changing. As our team member and payroll administrator, Sana Hajizada, shared so eloquently "Having a car gave me the wings to fly and get a job anywhere I wanted."

Another common investment is higher education. Many refugees, like Zinah and Werga, head back to school in pursuit of skills that will help them attain higher-paying or *more fulfilling* employment. While grants are often available to help, some, if not all of this expense comes out of their own pockets.

Some refugees are eager to leverage their funds to fulfill one of the great American dreams— homeownership. Amnobe and her family were among those. Her new employment gave them the financial boost they needed to quickly save for a down payment. When I sat down last year with Amnobe to hear her story, she communicated through her sister that they were under contract for a house. Buying a home is a *big deal* to anyone, but it was even more powerful for Amnobe. When they closed a few short weeks later, she was handed the keys to her first permanent home in over twenty years.

But earning money isn't all about making a better life for themself. The financial stability resulting from employment also gives them the ability to help provide for their families back home. Remember the community mindset I shared about briefly in chapter five? Many refugees who have been given the opportunity to resettle feel a sense of responsibility to the parents, grandparents, and siblings they left behind.

Regardless of the language, all refugees are united by one word: "hiwalla (hi-wall-uh)." Use this word in conversation with any refugee and you will garner an intriguing response. It refers to the process of sending money back home to care for loved ones.

The concept of pursuing a good job to send money back home to family is universal— no matter if they are from Africa or Southeast Asia, they will do what it takes to support their family. Sometimes this means frequent visits to Western Union, and other times it's dependent on a loose connection of trusted relationships to send money around the globe. Hiwalla is so fascinating to me and serves as a great example of the loyalty and resolve of the refugee workforce.

. . . .

Unlike her dead-end job at the chicken factory, Amnobe's new position afforded her opportunities to grow within the company. For the past year, she has shown up and worked hard to prove her ability.

Shortly after moving into their new home, Amnobe started English classes in hopes of being promoted. In the past year, she went from needing a translator to *being* a translator— a skill that is helping her company.

Her supervisor, Karina, has taken note of Amnobe's effort. More than fifty employees on her team are refugees, which Karina says is a big factor in her department's success. As someone who moved to the U.S. from another country and worked her way up from the bottom rung of the company, she now enjoys helping others do the same.

Yes, Karina offers Amnobe a promotion that comes with added responsibility. But it also comes with increased pay and valuable training.

Amnobe, of course, accepts.

Now she will lead a team of fellow employees, the second rung on the ladder she is climbing within the company.

The stability of a good job has given her the roots and resources to succeed. Now, she will do what she's always done: show up and perform her job with excellence, working toward the next opportunity.

. . . .

Acclimation

Every community has a culture, a way of life, and a certain set of social norms unlike anywhere else in the world.

I couldn't reside with a tribe in South America and still use my credit cards.

I couldn't move to England and continue to drive on the right side of the road.

And if I relocated to Afghanistan, I *certainly* couldn't give a "thumbs up" anymore (learned this one by mistake)!

To succeed in their new communities, refugees need to begin to get a feel for and begin acclimating to their surrounding culture. This happens by participation, not by hiding behind closed doors.

Refugees learn to engage with their new communities through jobs. Working builds confidence for them to begin participating in civic life, both inside and outside of work.

When I recently caught-up with Amnobe, she informed me (we carried on a full conversation over the phone without a translator!) she wanted to come into the office and talk. She said she has some ideas for Amplio to be able to provide insurance benefits to employees better suited for the refugee population —*I love that!*

A year ago, she was still trying to gain her footing. Now she's fully engaged and concerned with the well-being of her community, not just her own life.

For many refugees, employment is a giant leap into the "pool" of American culture. It takes a lot of courage, and once "inside," it takes time to get used to the temperature.

There are two areas where we most often see some initial conflict: time and hygiene. These are simple to overcome with upfront, tactful communication.

I've spent time in other parts of the world where life seems to move at a much slower pace. I can understand why many new arrivals are taken aback by our country's obsession with the big and little hands. The refugee workforce is eager to please, if they know what's expected of them. Communicate start and finish times and break guidelines, then cast the vision for why they are important.

And as for hygiene, it isn't just about showering regularly and using deodorant. It's also encouraging employees to wear a clean uniform to work every day. Deodorant is vital, but no amount of Axe body spray can cover up wearing clothes again that have already been sweat in for a few days in a row!

Skill Development
This is the catch-22 for many refugees: without marketable skills they cannot land a job, but without a job they have a harder time gaining valuable skills.

We've already discussed the appetite refugees have for learning. Employment gives them the opportunity to act on that hunger, and begin accumulating skills. The majority of skills gained at work are not only useful for the job at hand, but will also be attractive to future employers.

When one of our employees, Claudy, started at a landscaping company, they taught him how to mow, trim, mulch, and edge lawns. Those skills are not only serving him well at his current job, but will go with him into future positions at the company. He's also learning skills that will transfer into any career path such as attention to detail and how to exceed customer expectations.

In her new position, Amnobe is learning how to operate some of the manufacturing company's machinery. Since she plans to grow within the company, these skills will look great on her resume. Machines may vary from company to company, but the

> **JOBS ALLOW REFUGEES TO EXPAND THEIR SOCIAL NETWORK.**

intelligence and tenacity needed to learn them is the same.

Skill development is of little value without the right social network to help establish a career. This is another area where employment is beneficial. Jobs allow refugees to expand their social network. This is important because "refugees often lack contacts who can advise them on how to learn job-related skills, find work and pursue a particular career," revealed a Tent report.[83]

To an individual trying to establish a career, social contacts are key. The right connection can mean everything, and quite literally alter their path completely.

. . . .

Amnobe is an overcomer. Despite her tragic past, she manages her household, her children, and her job responsibilities with grace.
In just one year, she has made the monumental shift from surviving to thriving as a refugee in America.

She owns a house.
She is fluent in English.
She is moving up in her company.
She is gaining valuable skills and experience.
She is an advocate for positive change at work and within her community.

The catalyst for it all was simply *a good job.*

Amnobe is happy, and she is healing. *But she is not done.*

Now, she has set her sights on yet another dream: earning her GED. This next big step will enable her to continue to advance her career and provide more for her family.

Just as important, Amnobe knows going back to school will set an example for her daughters, ages one and seven. She hopes they, too, will work hard, learn all they can, and have a bright future.

. . . .

Healing

Refugees, like Amnobe, have more often than not suffered many unfathomable terrors - and great loss - by the time they resettle.

"The often traumatic reasons for leaving... as well as the potentially long and hazardous journey and process of resettlement increase the risk for refugees to suffer from a variety of mental health issues," one article on refugee health shares.[84]

While it is said, "Time heals all wounds," healing is more dependent on *what you do with that time.* Believe it or not, work is healthy. Meaningful activity plays a huge part in ongoing mental health and healing.

With the propensity toward mental illness, instigated by their experiences, it is even more imperative for refugees to re-enter the workforce quickly.

Unemployment is detrimental to even the healthiest mind, let alone one that has endured great instability and loss. "There is a strong association between worklessness and poor health," a study by the Centre for Health and Social Care Research explains. The study linked unemployment to higher mortality, illness, psychological distress, medication consumption, and even hospital admission.[85]

Oppositely, employment has many health benefits, *especially for refugees.*

The stability of a job reduces anxiety, and provides space for refugees to begin the process of recovery. It's hard to focus on healing when you don't know where your next meal is going to come from. As Bethelhem often shares, "A good job is peace of mind."

Shortly after starting her job with us at Amplio, she showed us some of her personal paintings. She told us that she had not painted since leaving her home in Ethiopia. But now, after feeling the peace and joy born out of employment, she had gone out and bought some supplies and was painting again. I absolutely love seeing all of Betty's exceptional artwork. I think it's a metaphor for the flourishing possible within an entire community when there is stable employment.

Amnobe, too, had talent lying dormant. She was a very popular singer back home in Congo before being displaced. She recently has re-engaged her passion for singing and now has over 70,000 views on Youtube! The healing that employment affords individuals like Betty and Amnobe allows them to flourish and be fully themselves again.[*]

Every day resettled individuals from all around the world step into our offices across the U.S. looking for a job. More often than not, their heads are down, and their shoulders slumped, their body language expressing their inner sense of hopelessness.

To them, the beginning of a job is often the beginning of hope— faith that life can be better than what they have experienced and are experiencing.

After starting a job, small "wins" at work give these individuals a sense of accomplishment, which also serves to combat depression. And utilizing their talents can help them discover their passions and give them *purpose.*

---

[*] Visit **www.refugeeworkforce.com** to check out Betty's art and Amnobe's music videos!

Something else to note here is that healthy communities are made up of healthy individuals. A person who is employed positively affects their entire community. A rising tide lifts all ships. An individual who is thriving will help others do the same, and break the cycle of poverty that is prevalent in refugee communities.

Dignity

In this chapter, I've talked us through a few of the many benefits of employment for refugees. We started with the most obvious— security and income. Now I would like to end with one of the most overlooked but deeply meaningful aspects of having a job: dignity.

There is a clear connection between dignity and work. As Pope John Paul II put it, "man's life is built up every day for work, from work it derives its specific dignity…"[86]

While every human being is innately worthy of love and respect, one's ability to contribute (or not) to society can distort this truth.

As much as we long for vacations and joke about retiring, we *need* work as an essential part of the human experience.

Without work (paid or unpaid), individuals lose their sense of pride, and suffer from low self-esteem. Mandah Chimgeew, a refugee from East Asia, expressed, "As a refugee, I felt like people saw me as a beggar. Nobody saw me that way, but it was my mindset."

Mandah was right. Nobody saw her as a beggar. But without a way to contribute, she saw herself that way.

Many refugees endure *years* of being unable to work (because of living in host countries) and relying on others to meet their needs, resulting in a palpable sense of shame. For them, the ability to work, be self-reliant, and give back to their communities serves as an important function in restoring their lost dignity.

"In addition to providing an income, work makes refugees feel valued and proud that they are giving something back,"[87] and those feelings translate to confidence.

This confidence quickly extends into other areas of life, like in the case of Amnobe. Think about it: while shame makes you want to hide, confidence gives you the courage to go out and attempt more. Refugees who have dignity are ready to go out and fully engage at work and in their communities.

I think it's great how much research has been conducted on how companies can benefit from hiring refugees. At the same time, it's pathetic to realize how little attention has been brought to the benefits of those jobs for refugees.

> **THE BEST WAY TO HELP REFUGEES IN THE LONG RUN IS NOT MORE HANDOUTS, BUT CONNECTING THEM TO SKILLS TRAINING AND VIABLE JOBS WITHIN THE MARKET.**

I'm grateful that there are so many organizations and programs to help resettle individuals and provide access to information and basic necessities.

However, the best way to help refugees in the long run is not more handouts, but connecting them to skills training and viable jobs within the market.

Jobs help refugees regain a sense of security and dignity. Income enables them to build capital, and attain their dreams. Immersion in the American workplace helps refugees to socially assimilate more quickly, and promotes emotional healing.

Refugees benefit their employers. Employment benefits refugees.

We've spent the last seven chapters laying out a clear case. Now, as we wind down this book, it's time to consider what action we must take.

- What bridges can we build to better engage the full potential of the refugee workforce?

- How do we leverage policy for greater economic impact?

- What does the future of refugee resettlement look like for the U.S.?

- How can we best invest our financial resources to better serve the refugee workforce while positioning companies for growth?

In our final chapter together, I'll share some innovative approaches companies, nonprofits and both local and foreign governments are taking. Together, we'll dream about what can happen when we intentionally build-out a model to support both refugees and local businesses.

EIGHT | A BRIGHTER FUTURE

*"We realized we needed to put the plant
where the labor force is."*

When Jim and Nancy Konides moved their family to Atlanta, the plan was to open a self-serve laundromat that would improve upon the traditional model. Jim had been selling his proprietary zero-trace laundry solution to hotels and other commercial businesses for over 25 years. Now, he would bring that eco-friendly washing service straight to the consumer through a new business he called "Blusion."

"At the last minute, we decided to staff the laundromat," Jim shares about how their trajectory shifted. "We needed money to pay the staff, so we started offering a wash, dry and fold service."

The decision turned out to be a good one. The combination of Blusion's affordable price point plus the expanding economy led to high demand. "People were begging us to do their laundry. That was so weird to me," shares Nancy. Weird or not, It wasn't long before they were looking for ways to grow the wash-dry-fold end of their business.

"That's when we came up with the locker idea," Jim explains. The idea? Install smart, weatherproof laundry lockers everywhere from apartment homes, to hospitals, to universities.

The couple began working with a world-leader in locker innovation from Australia. They developed fully-automated indoor-outdoor lockers that could be placed at any convenient location. When customers place dirty laundry in a locker, it's retrieved by a Blusion team member, then taken to a central laundry facility. There, they use their patented system to deep-clean each item of clothing. Once clean, the garments are dried, folded, and placed neatly back into the original locker— all within the short span of 48 hours.

Jim and Nancy put a lot of care into developing every piece of equipment, every process and procedure of the business. Their commitment to excellence led to great success, and success led to more expansion. However, as usually happens, the company's expansion came with a new set of problems. For them, it was finding, *and keeping,* dependable workers to fill the added positions.

"From day one, we had an informal consultant that kept saying, 'Your number one problem is going to be labor,'" Jim explains. The prediction was accurate.

"The economy had a lot to do with it," Jim shares. "We've had a lot of great people, and some great experiences— and we love that side of it. But we were struggling to find people. Last year I was really questioning the whole business model—*can we expand this?"*

The couple knew the business had the potential to grow exponentially, but without good employees, they just weren't getting the traction they needed. About that time, a friend, Jeff Pack in Nashville, brought to their attention a new idea, a labor pool previously unconsidered by Jim and Nancy: *the refugee workforce.*

Jim met with Amplio Recruiting to begin exploring solutions. After Amplio placed just a few refugee employees, Jim and Nancy began to see a noticeable difference.

"The employees are so intuitive," Jim shares. "There's not a lot of over-managing. They care."

"In the beginning it was just my daughter and myself, working to make sure every customer had the same experience," Nancy chimes in. "We had to put our hands in everything. Now we don't have to do that. The job isn't like washing hospital linens, where you're going to do the same thing the same way. The pieces are different. It's very strategic. We coach them on thinking through the process. Their performance is important to them, personally. They see a problem coming, and they'll say something."

Their refugee employees not only carry-out Blusion's commitment to excellence, but they take initiative, and responsibility for their actions. And Jim and Nancy are grateful for more than just their exceptional performance— the relationships they've built are invaluable to them.

Dubbed Blusion "mom," Nancy keeps up with the ins and outs of their lives—

Lois is going to school to be a dental hygienist.

Irene is working hard to create a better future for her small kids.

Mohammad is "not a big talker," Nancy admits, but the young man's hard work does the talking for him.

It was only a year ago that they first began to explore the idea of hiring refugees. Today the Konides family couldn't imagine Blusion without them. The difference these employees have made has been so positive and impactful, it has entirely changed the Blusion strategic growth plan.

"What's nice about our model is that we can locate our plant (the central laundry facility where the wash-dry-fold occurs) anywhere—not everyone can do that.

Originally we were thinking wherever the most customers would be is where we should put it. But we realized we needed to put the plant where the labor force is."

. . . .

If you've stuck with me until now, I hope you're as excited as I am about the potential of the refugee workforce.

The labor shortage crisis is a huge problem. The refugee crisis is a huge problem. But together, they make one big positive win-win solution.

> **"WE REALIZED WE NEEDED TO PUT THE PLANT WHERE THE LABOR FORCE IS."**

I wasn't the first to recognize the refugee value, and I'm certainly not the only one doing something about it. I've mentioned several fantastic businesses and organizations in this book making great strides when it comes to more effective refugee integration.

In our final pages together, I want to share a few more. The goal is to inspire you; and to awaken your imagination. I hope these stories cause you to consider how you, your business, your passions, your experiences, and your people might come together to form new, innovative solutions.

We know refugee employees are good for companies, and employment is good for refugees. **So how can we better help refugees access living-wage jobs utilizing their talents, intellect, and experiences?**

Let's start with a small-scale picture, and look at a few companies taking action.

Company Level

At Amplio, we have the privilege of working with some amazing clients (some of whom I've already mentioned). As a result of our work, we are often invited into refugee workforce discussions with some of the greatest changemakers within the marketplace. There's not enough room left in this book to tell you about all of them. So for now I'll just share a few to get your wheels turning.

Figure 8 is an investment advisory firm based in Boise, Idaho. When it was launched in 2016, Figure 8 set out to build a team of investment analysts to guide its global strategy. They sought individuals with deep knowledge of key economic sectors, a strong understanding of geopolitical and cultural trends, and multilingual skills. It just so happened they found that talent in Boise's refugee and immigrant communities.

Now, Figure 8's investment team hails from four different continents, speaks seven languages, and provides smart and disciplined investment management for the firm's increasingly diverse client base. A doctor from Iraq, an engineer from Burma, and a professor from Rwanda don't walk into a bar— they walk into Figure 8's offices with their heads held high, ready for another day of analyzing investment opportunities around the world.

Tazikis Mediterranean Cafe is a nationwide quick-service franchise growing in popularity. Their goal is to have experienced chefs in every kitchen, despite the industry's reputation for high turnover resulting from low pay. To accomplish this goal, Tazikis decided to forge a new path. They made a commitment to provide living wage salaries and benefits for kitchen staff. That single decision has allowed them to recruit and retain some incredibly talented chefs in their restaurants— among them, many individuals from the refugee workforce.

As demand rose, Tazikis CEO, Dan Simpson, began to consider new ways of recruiting talent. That's when he connected with Luke Keller to learn more about hiring refugees in his restaurants. He and his team recognized many refugees, resettling legally in the U.S., grew up cooking and enjoying Mediterranean cuisine. That experience, they believed, would make them exceptional "chefugees" in Tazikis restaurants across the country.

Now, they are taking a bold step, just as Starbucks, WeWork and Hilton have done before them. They intend to launch a national hiring campaign for refugees and we're very excited to help them with this endeavor.

LeadGenius is a sales research and lead generation firm based in Berkley, California. They are a tech giant employing remote workers around the world to provide in-depth analysis and research for big name clients including Google, Facebook, Amazon, and Salesforce.

Founder Prayag Narula believes in the power of software to make a more equitable world, and has built the business around that vision. That has led LeadGenius to adapt their training program, allowing them to provide refugees with online, personal growth and living wage employment. Here's the crazy part—they're not just doing it here in the U.S. LeadGenius is now aiming to employ refugees around the world, many of whom are stuck in refugee camps.

In many parts of the world, host countries don't allow refugees to take local jobs; however remote employment is permissible under migrant law. Following Prayag's careful direction LeadGenius hopes to graduate 200 refugees from their upcoming pilot training program and build toward *20,000* graduates one day. That's 20,000 refugees who will be trained in valuable tech skills, and have the opportunity to obtain greater stability for themselves and their families.

Blusion's story, woven here, is quickly becoming one of my favorites. A year ago, refugees were absent from Jim and Nancy's radar— now their entire business is being built around them. Recognizing both the social and economic benefits, they've shifted their company model. Now, the six plus regional plants they hope to establish in the coming years will all be strategically placed in refugee communities.

That single shift will create between 500 to 1,000 living wage jobs for refugees, while eliminating the hurdle of transportation. But Nancy, who remembers what it's like to raise three small children, says she wants to take it one step further.

"I would love to create a way to provide childcare," she shares. "These parents need to go to work, but they're thinking, 'What can I do with my kid?' To be able to provide amazing care—that's what's in my head."

What about your company?

- What experiences do refugees have that might meet a specific need in your place of business?

- What training program could you implement that could fill any skills gap between what potential employees know and what you need?

> IF MORE BUSINESS LEADERS TOOK THE TIME TO STOP AND CONSIDER WHAT THEY COULD DO, THE SOCIAL AND ECONOMICAL IMPACT WOULD BE TREMENDOUS.

- Is there flexibility to shift your company's model to better engage the refugee community? Or is there a way to help with transportation to your facility?

Take a moment to consider these questions. The answers just might surprise you. If more business leaders took the time to stop and consider what they could do (instead of what they can't), the social and economical impact would be tremendous.

. . . .

With his new expansion plan in mind, Jim turned his focus back to producing their state-of-the-art lockers. He began negotiations with a Chinese manufacturing firm; however, just when he was ready to sign the contract and get production rolling, a news article alerted him to a catastrophic development.

The U.S.-China trade war had elevated. President Trump announced tariff increases on $200 billion worth of Chinese imports. China responded by putting levies on U.S. goods to the tune of $60 billion.[88]

Trump's stroke of the pen caused a massive increase in production costs, which would cut deeply into Blusion's gross profit projections.

Instead of a one percent tax, he now had to pay 25 percent in taxes— an increase of $3,000 per unit. *The cost would hang Blusion out to dry.*

It would make sense for anyone to despair in such a situation—but not Jim and Nancy. Instead, they turned their attention back to the refugee community. At Amplio's suggestion, they met with Tekton Career Training, an Atlanta-based nonprofit equipping men and women with skilled trades training.

They knew refugees made a dependable workforce for washing and folding laundry, but could they also help them with building tech-enabled lockers?

Tekton's electrical and assembly training seemed like the perfect place to execute Blusion's locker assembly plans. Students could continue training, and get paid for work while gaining valuable resume experience and honing their craft.

After discussions, Tekton and Blusion formed a partnership. Soon, a small team representing very different cultures and languages will begin to assemble lockers in Clarkston.

Jim and Nancy couldn't be more grateful for, and excited about the partnership. "We're blown away by the ingenuity of this community. When we have a problem, they have a solution. We can't wait to see how this partnership unfolds over the next few years."

. . . .

Organizational Level
Now that we've seen how individuals are making an impact at a company level, let's look at how some organizations are taking action as well.

As the trade war escalates, filling manufacturing shortages is becoming increasingly imperative.

At Amplio, we have the privilege of partnering with many organizations who have already recognized this growing need, and are shifting their approach to more quickly move refugees into these key positions.

Tekton Career Training is a great example of an organization making a big impact in this area. We touched on their work above, and in Chapter Five featuring Werga. Similar to my experience, Luke Keller also saw two needs and considered how he could play a part in bringing them together. The result was a training model that is not only effective, but highly scalable.

Tekton Career training provides inexpensive skills development that is simultaneously engaging refugees and meeting the demand for skilled tradesmen in the marketplace. Remember the stat we mentioned in the "IF Gap" section in Chapter One? Ten thousand boomers are retiring per day and younger generations are not picking up the slack, especially in skilled trades.[89]

For-profit and nonprofit partnerships, like the one between Blusion and Tekton, set a great example of how collaboration can help everyone involved achieve their goals.[*]

The Tent Partnership for Refugees was launched by Hamdi Ulukaya who immigrated to the U.S. and founded a Greek yogurt company called "Chobani." Tent's mission is to collaborate with other global brands to provide employment opportunities for refugees, and resources for the companies hiring them.

Leading companies including Google, Starbucks, Hilton, Facebook, Deloitte and Microsoft are all proud members of The Tent Partnership. Amplio was invited into this exclusive group in 2017, and has benefited greatly from the collaboration.

---

[*] Visit **www.refugeeworkforce.com** for our interview with Luke Keller and Laura Green of Tekton Career Training.

Tent convenes companies engaging the refugee crisis head on. Their ongoing research is an invaluable resource to members and, in fact, has been used frequently throughout this book.

Welcoming America is growing a movement by helping communities in the U.S. foster a culture of inclusion for immigrants and refugees. The private sector, both small businesses and large corporations play a huge role in this effort.

Through coaching, consultations, and assessments, Welcoming America is building more prosperous and vibrant communities. Some communities have taken the step to become "Welcoming Certified" by undergoing a rigorous assessment, including in-person audits. Clarkston, Georgia (the smallest city in process) and Dallas, Texas (the largest city in process) are joined by many others including Pittsburgh, Cincinnati, Baltimore and Charlotte in their pursuit.[*] Welcoming America hopes many more cities, big and small, will join the welcoming movement in the coming years.

State + Country Level
Policy is being shaped at the state-level as well. Let's look at what some are doing when it comes to lowering barriers pertaining to immigrant and refugee employment.

As a born-and-raised Georgia resident, I'm proud of steps being taken by our state to more intentionally engage the refugee workforce. Recently I began working with the **Small Business Committee of the Georgia House of Representatives** to create a sub-committee aimed at refugee and immigrant workforce development. The group will be comprised of political representatives and refugee advocates who have direct access to propose new legislation. And while I originally battled with the idea of forming another "pointless" committee, I have come to realize how beneficial it is for our community to have such a direct connection to shaping policy.

---

[*] For an audio interview with Dallas city manager about the crucial role of immigrants in the vitality of their city, visit our book website at **www.refugeeworkforce.com**.

Instead of simply being *reactive* to what is perceived as bad policy, our community can *proactively* propose ideas for new legislation. While we're just getting started here in Georgia, we're inspired by other states taking action.

Washington has established a "Keep Washington Working" workgroup which conducts ongoing research to innovate new ways to strengthen career pathways for immigrants.

New Jersey has formed a first-of-its-kind "Office of New Americans" that will focus on immigrant and refugee resettlement, integration, and job placement initiatives.[90]

Massachusetts is working toward making the licensing and credentialing process easier to navigate for new arrivals. For example, a refugee who worked as a medical professional back in their home country can be expedited through the licensure process if they are willing to practice in certain rural communities.

> **INSTEAD OF BEING REACTIVE TO WHAT IS PERCEIVED AS BAD POLICY, COMMUNITIES CAN PROACTIVELY PROPOSE IDEAS FOR NEW LEGISLATION.**

Visit our book website at **www.refugeeworkforce.com** where you can find a list of past legislation relating to refugee and immigrant employment.

Now, let's zoom out and expand our view to look at what some countries are doing to expedite the immigration process for refugees in need, and lower their barriers to employment.

Canadian entrepreneur Jim Estill made a name for himself when he sponsored over 200 refugees to resettle in his hometown, the southwestern Ontario town of Guelph. Frustrated by a lack of response to the Syrian crisis, Jim began searching for a way to help.

That was when he learned about the **Canadian private refugee sponsorship program**. The program allows private citizens to sponsor refugees' resettlement by providing basic needs and helping them integrate. Jim knew, in order to do this quickly, that he would need to collaborate. He partnered with ten different organizations who, over the course of a year, helped 47 families. When many of these newcomers struggled to find employment, Jim took it a step further, and started a program to teach them English skills and provide opportunities to work at his company, Danby, an appliance manufacturing company. [91]

Jim's only hope is that others will follow his example and take action. Canada's concept of allowing the private sector to participate directly in immigration is groundbreaking, and will have a positive effect not only for the sponsored refugees, but within the overall economy. I love the concept of the private sector leading the responsibility for resettlement rather than the burden relying solely on the government.

Brazil's voluntary relocation initiative officially launched in April 2018 as a response to the Venzuelan refugee crisis that has forced over four million individuals to flee due to hyperinflation and political instability.[92] Many Venezuelans resettled in North Brazil, putting a strain on host communities. In response, Brazil began working with UNHCR to identify eligible beneficiaries, who are then relocated to one of over fifty participating cities and placed into jobs in private companies.[93]

Within a few short months, the initiative has helped relocate over 5,000 Venezuelans, and has been heralded by the UN as one of the most innovative responses to the refugee crisis in decades.

As I work on this final chapter, I'm physically sitting inside of a refugee camp on the Venezuelan/Colombian border. The Colombian government, much like Brazil has recognized the economic value refugees can have for their nation and have created innovative policies to allow individuals from Venezuela to enter the workforce as soon as possible.

(Check out the resource page for several short video updates of my time at the Colombian border and how we can apply potential solutions to the crisis at our own border.)[*]

I should also note that I'm encouraged by the recent formation of the **American Workforce Policy Advisory Board**, made up of 25 highly successful and respected business leaders. Their goal is to come up with innovative solutions to current employment challenges facing U.S. businesses. Among many tasks at hand, one is creating better paths to employment for refugees and documented immigrants.

We still have a lot to learn, but progress is being made. At the time of this writing, our team continues to find more up-to-date news articles alerting us to new, positive developments around the globe.

. . . .

This is where the story comes full circle, and collides with my own.

Around the same time Jim Konides reached out to us about their labor shortage problem at Blusion, I had been dreaming of ways we could make an even greater impact on a global scale through Amplio.

We had already set a huge goal of 25 locations across the U.S. by 2025, which would result in placing an estimated 30,000 refugees into jobs, and take us to $100 million in revenue. But as I heard reports of 70 million displaced people around the world without stability, I realized we were only touching a tiny fraction of the global crisis defining our generation.

I began to ask dangerous questions, such as "How do we move the needle to help the *millions* in flux?"

---

[*] **www.refugeeworkforce.com/resources**

Our original model would work well in developed nations, such as the U.S. and Europe. However, job placement would not be effective in developing economies. We had to turn our attention to job creation.

With that thought in mind, I helped launch a venture capital firm along with partners, Chase Carroll and Dalton T. Sirmans. The purpose of Amplio Ventures is to invest in refugee entrepreneurs and companies intentionally employing refugees on a global scale. Up to this point, we have never taken a capital investment for Amplio Recruiting because of strong cash flow, but many of the individuals wanting to back us were interested in investing in other "refugee-powered" businesses through Amplio Ventures.

Once Amplio Ventures was formed and looking to make its first investment, we reached out to Jim and Nancy at Blusion. I was captivated by their vision to grow and saw how we could help them with the capital needed to achieve their desired level of scale and impact. Jim was not interested in traditional financing from an institution, but he was very open to aligned capital from people he could trust with a similar vision.

As a result, Amplio Ventures was thrilled to make its very first investment— in Blusion.[*]

Now, our firm is engaged with over 20 companies, and growing, including LeadGenius, which I mentioned above. Together, we're launching the Remote Refugee Employment Fund.[*] We've combined low-risk, high-yield U.S.-based companies to employ high-risk, high-yield refugees in camps around the world. The end goal is that any refugee with a device and Wi-Fi connection will have access to training, and a connection to the global marketplace.

---

[*] Visit **www.refugeeworkforce.com** for an informational video about Blusion

[*] Visit **www.refugeeworkforce.com** for a link to more information about the Remote Refugee Employment Fund.

· · · · · · · · · · ·

While this feels like the end, it is really just the beginning of a bigger story. A story I hope many more individuals, for-profits, nonprofits and governments will be a part of.

The refugee crisis is one of the defining issues of our generation and it poses an overwhelming, unrelenting challenge. I believe collaboration and innovation can lead us to a better future than any of us could ever achieve on our own.

As we close out, I want to leave you with this thought: big or small, every action taken to better integrate refugees into our workforce is a win for companies, a win for refugees, and a win for the overall economy.

It's easy to become so overwhelmed by the enormity of the refugee crisis, or the enormity of the labor shortage problem that we neglect to ask, "What part can I play in the solution?"

I shared at the beginning of this book, that I'm no hero, but I have the honor of working with a lot of them. I am an average guy who was willing to move beyond awareness, to take action. That's a responsibility I believe each of us have as humans who care about our fellow man. We no longer have the option of standing on the sidelines.

Whatever idea or conviction you have, press into it. Lean into the discomfort, and say "yes"— *you never know where it might take you.*

If nothing is tugging at you just yet, it's worth reading the conclusion. I've tucked some simple ideas in there that can help you know how to take action.

On we go!

CONCLUSION

If you were here, I'd introduce you to our incredibly talented team. They're tucked in every corner of our humble office, doing the hard work that makes the stories you've read a reality every week.

You'd meet good-humored Sana, from Afghanistan, who fought alongside U.S. troops in Kabul. He oversees the crucial job of managing payroll for 300+ employees. He's been with us for nearly three years and his attention to detail often saves us from making big mistakes.

Betty, from Ethiopia, is our soft-spoken powerhouse. At any given moment you can find her translating English, Amharic and French, as she helps individuals fill-out applications for what is often their first job here in America.

Zinah, whom you met earlier, has a contagious smile and sits behind three computer screens. She monitors and organizes data, keeping us moving forward efficiently (all while pursuing her next big goal of obtaining her PhD).

Yonten, from Bhutan, is joyful and intuitive. He helps prepare and place dependable refugees into jobs that will be a good fit for them. He's easily the most patient person in the office and is confrontational in all the right ways.

I would introduce you to Luke and Stephen, who contribute critically with herculean efforts. Luke is diligent and upbeat as he leads our sales and expansion, while Stephen manages the Atlanta office with his humility and perseverance.

Our office buzzes with a steady stream of people coming and going, conversations in different languages, and the tapping of fingers on keyboards— the soundtrack of a team committed to helping *more* great companies connect with the dependable refugee workforce in the coming years.

We have an audacious goal of placing 30,000 refugees into full-time employment in the U.S. by 2025. It's going to require partnering with other passionate people who are willing to take action.[*]

This is where I extend an invitation to you— to become a part of that mission.

Here's what we've learned in our time together:

- With 7.5 million open jobs and only 5.8 million individuals looking, there is room for anyone who is willing to work. Refugees are not taking jobs from Americans, rather they are meeting a great need.

- Resettled refugees are not only legal to work, they are *eager to work,* making them some of the most dependable and hard-working employees a company will ever have.

- Hiring the dependable refugee workforce will help repair the "flat tire" cycle of high turnover many companies are facing, leading to higher productivity, retention, and profit.

---

[*] To request information about becoming an owner/operator of an Amplio Recruiting office in your city visit **www.ampliorecruiting.com/owneroperator**.

The diversity and growth mindset refugees bring creates an added layer of benefits including increased innovation, improved morale, access to a wider range of talent, and more.

- Employment is the best way to help refugees. It provides the foundation for refugees to put down roots, regain a sense of security, and rebuild their lives.

There will be many individuals who read this book and relegate the evidence herein to nothing more than an intriguing idea. But my hope is there will be many more who take this information and *do something about it.*

John F. Kennedy once said, "There are risks and costs to action. But they are far less than the long range risks of comfortable inaction."[94]

Inaction, in the case of hiring the displaced, will come at a literal cost to our great nation. Companies will continue to fight the "flat tire cycle" of undependable employees; the gap between the number of workers we *have* versus the number of workers we *need* will continue to grow; and the economy will most assuredly stall. Meanwhile, we will continue to dump millions of taxpayers' dollars into initiatives, attempting to fix the "leak," while the solution is kept at arm's length.

Inaction will also cost our new neighbors, refugees and immigrants, who will continue to struggle, and whose potential will remain locked inside of them. It will cost them more than money— it will cost them their dreams, their dignity, their healing, and their healthy integration back into society. And if we continue down our current path of lessening immigration (because of fear and an overall lack of understanding), it will also cost lives.

What, then, is our cost of action?

Action will cost us some time, for one. And certainly some effort. It will cost us a little pride, when we have to give up our age-old ways of doing things.

It might cost a few friends, connections— or even employees— when we decide to take a stand on such a polarizing issue.

But Chris, you might still be asking, *is it worth all that?*
I believe with all my heart and my wallet that yes, it is.

Building better bridges for refugees to move efficiently into the American workplace attacks several key problem areas at once. First, and most obvious, it would provide hurting industries with the help they so desperately need right now.

With fewer labor shortages, suppliers would be able to meet demand and nurture a growing economy. Then, as businesses become unstuck, they would be able to channel their energies into innovating new products and services. Added to all this is the fact that more individuals working means more tax dollars being paid into the system. While, at the same time, the burden on said system would become less and less as more immigrant families become self-sufficient.

The potential is *undeniably huge.*

So where do we go from here? After all, information is great, but it's in the *application* that change happens.

Big dreams happen one step at a time, so here are a few simple steps we can all take, starting today:

- Hire refugees, or talk to your employer about the value refugees could bring to your company.

- Buy some copies of this book for business owners who could benefit from the refugee workforce.

- Contact your local representatives, urging them to increase the number of refugees allowed to seek asylum in the U.S.

Visit our book website for a great resource to share that includes eight reasons why the refugee workforce is the best kept secret for America's economy.

- Support refugee entrepreneurs and local businesses that hire from within the refugee community.[*]

- Befriend a refugee family in your community or search "refugee organizations near me" to find a local service provider and learn how you can volunteer.

- Offer to be a reference for a refugee applying for work.

- Purchase educational books, stories, and memoirs about the refugee crisis.

Orlando, Kelly, Jim, Nancy, Luke, Stephen and myself may have all stumbled into the idea of the refugee workforce, but we would all tell you— we're glad we said "yes." It is not just our businesses that are better— our *lives* are better for knowing and engaging with extraordinary people like Mohammad, Werga, Amnobe, Sana, Bethelhem, Zinah, Yonten and so many others.

Whether you stumbled into this book by accident, or you've been anxiously awaiting its release, thank you for taking the time to read and engage this discussion with an open mind. You now have the incredible opportunity to be a part of the solution to two great needs.

Will you say "yes" to the refugee workforce?

---

[*] Visit **www.refugeeworkforce.com** for a list of companies that have signed the wehirerefugees.org pledge.

ACKNOWLEDGMENTS

This book is dedicated to the 70 million displaced individuals around the globe, and especially to the more than 5,000 we've employed over the past 5 years.

The stories in this book would not be possible without the herculean efforts of our incredible team, Luke Keller, Stephen Assink, Sana Hajizada, Betty Bidiglen, Yonten Basnet, Zinah Ghazi, San Nuam, and so many others who've contributed in huge ways, especially those who have helped us trailblaze in new markets. *Thank you!*

Special thanks to the 300+ clients we've had the pleasure of serving, and the numerous non-profit partners we lock arms with everyday.

This book would still be nothing more than an item on my to-do list if it weren't for the writing prowess of Katie Gibson. Her patience with me and commitment to this project has been astounding. Katie's natural talent along with the research chops of Tyler White and strong support from Sophie Stoddard made up the dream team. I'm very grateful for each of you.

To our editorial team, who took our work and made it so much better— thank you to Dalton and Margie Sirmans, San Nuam, Mohammad Soda, Zeba Parvez and my mom, Becky Chancey.

I'm grateful for the support of my family, Sarah and Boaz, who gave me the time, space, and sounding board I needed to start AND finish this project.

Lastly, I'm humbled and grateful the Lord has allowed me to be surrounded by such amazing people and produce this work "for such a time as this."

-Chris

THE AUTHORS

Chris Chancey is the CEO of Amplio Recruiting, which he founded in 2014 to connect resettled refugees with open positions in the Atlanta job market. In the past five years, Amplio has grown steadily, helping over 300 companies fill crucial labor shortages with the "refugee workforce." Amplio now operates in five U.S. cities and counting, including Houston, Dallas, Detroit and Raleigh, in addition to Atlanta. Chris has enthusiastically engaged thousands of individuals at events including SOCAP, Q Commons, Lions Den and Praxis Labs, and multiple churches and universities annually.

Chris is the author and editor for Bible on Business, a faith & work devotional with readership of over 25,000. He has also written for, or been featured by NPR, Inc.com, Fast Company, Univision, Monster.com, The Atlanta Journal Constitution, Christianity Today and The Institute for Faith, Work and Economics.

Chris resides in Atlanta, Georgia with his wife, Sarah, and their son, Boaz.

Katie Gibson is a creative writer, author, and Bible teacher. As marketing coordinator for Amplio, she tells the stories of refugees and the companies who hire them, and shares deep insights into the resettlement process. With twelve years of experience in the non-profit sector, she believes in the power of story to move individuals to positive action.

Katie is the author of children's book, "Different by Design," and blogs about faith, marriage, and motherhood at **www.katiegibsonwrites.com**

Katie resides in Atlanta, Georgia with her husband, Craig, and their three   children

NOTES

Introduction

[1] "Refugee Statistics," USA for UNHCR, accessed May 10, 2019, **Introduction** unrefugees.org/refugee-facts/statistics/.

[2] "Refugee Statistics," USA for UNHCR, accessed May 10, 2019, https://www.unrefugees.org/refugee-facts/statistics/.

[2] "Figures at a Glance." UNHCR. Accessed June 24, 2019. https://www.unhcr.org/en-us/figures-at-a-glance.html.

[3] "Job Openings and Labor Turnover Summary," Economic News Release, U.S. Bureau of Labor Statistics, last modified May 7, 2019, https://www.bls.gov/news.release/archives/jolts_05072019.htm.

[4] "Employment Situation Summary." U.S. Bureau of Labor Statistics, May 3, 2019. https://www.bls.gov/news.release/archives/empsit_05032019.htm.

Chapter One

[5] "Job Openings and Labor Turnover Summary," Economic News Release, U.S. Bureau of Labor Statistics, last modified May 7, 2019, https://www.bls.gov/news.release/archives/jolts_05072019.htm ; "Employment Situation Summary," Economic News Release, U.S. Bureau of Labor Statistics, last modified May 3, 2019, https://www.bls.gov/news.release/archives/empsit_05032019.htm.

[6] Ilan Brat, "On U.S. Farms, Fewer Hands for the Harvest," *Wall Street Journal*, updated August 12, 2015, https://www.wsj.com/articles/on-u-s-farms-fewer-hands-for-the-harvest-1439371802.

[7] Mandy Mitchell, "Construction Worker Poaching Adds to Triangle's Rising Home Prices," WRAL.com, posted May 4, 2018, https://www.wral.com/construction-worker-poaching-adds-to-triangle-s-rising-home-prices/17531772/.

[8] Kristen Korosec, "America's Trucker Shortage Is Hitting Home," *Fortune*, June 27, 2018, http://fortune.com/2018/06/27/americas-trucker-shortage/.

[9] Rick Barrett, "Growing Fast, a Small Wisconsin Manufacturer Turns Business Away Because of Labor Shortage," *Journal Sentinel* (Milwaukee), updated October 17, 2018, https://www.jsonline.com/story/money/2018/10/17/growing-fast-small-manufacturer-turns-business-away-because-labor-shortage/1668476002/.

[10] Glenn Kessler, "Do 10,000 Baby Boomers Retire Every Day?" *Washington Post*, July 24, 2014, https://www.washingtonpost.com/news/fact-checker/wp/2014/07/24/do-10000-baby-boomers-retire-every-day/?utm_term=.39dd6862c05d.; Anthony P. Carnevale, Nicole Smith, and Jeff Strohl, "Recovery: Job Growth and Education Requirements through 2020," Center on Education and the Workforce, Georgetown University, accessed July 10, 2019, https://cew.georgetown.edu/cew-reports/recovery-job-growth-and-education-requirements-through-2020/.

[11] Jeffrey S. Passel and D'Vera Cohn, "Unauthorized Immigrant Workforce Is Smaller," Pew Research Center Hispanic Trends, November 27, 2018, https://www.pewhispanic.org/2018/11/27/unauthorized-immigrant-workforce-is-smaller-but-with-more-women/.

[12] Michael D. Farren and Scott Winship, "Supply or Demand? What's the Story behind Men Leaving the Labor Force?," Mercatus Center, George Mason University, May 1, 2018, https://www.mercatus.org/essays/men-leaving-labor-force-supply-demand.

[13] Didem Tüzemen, "Why Are Prime-Age Men Vanishing from the Labor Force?" *The Federal Reserve Bank of Kansas City Economic Review*, First Quarter 2018: 6, https://doi.org/10.18651/er/1q18tuzemen

[14] Farren and Winship, "Supply or Demand?"

[15] Melissa Wylie, "Surprising Stats on Drugs in the Workplace," Psychemedics, January 29, 2018, https://www.psychemedics.com/blog/2018/01/surprising-stats-drugs-workplace/; "Drug Testing Index," Quest Diagnostics, accessed May 10, 2019, https://www.questdiagnostics.com/home/physicians/health-trends/drug-testing/table1.html.

[16] Nathan N. O'Hara, Andrew N. Pollak, Christopher J. Welsh, et al., "Factors Associated with Persistent Opioid Use Among Injured Workers' Compensation Claimants," *JAMA Network Open,* 1, no. 6 (October 26, 2018), https://doi.org/10.1001/jamanetworkopen.2018.4050.

[17] "Opioid Overdose Crisis," National Institute on Drug Abuse, revised January 22, 2019, https://www.drugabuse.gov/drugs-abuse/opioids/opioid-overdose-crisis.

.

[18] Scott Stump, "'One America': Small Town Welcomes Thousands of Refugees with Southern Hospitality," *Today*, July 3, 2018, https://www.today.com/news/clarkston-georgia-home-thousands-refugees-t132421

[19] "Clarkston, GA," Data USA, accessed May 10, 2019, https://datausa.io/profile/geo/clarkston-ga/. .

[20] U.S. Bureau of Labor Statistics, "Job Openings and Labor Turnover."

[21] U.S. Bureau of Labor Statistics, "Job Openings and Labor Turnover."

[22] "How the Government Measures Unemployment," Labor Force Statistics from the Current Population Survey, U.S. Bureau of Labor Statistics, last modified October 8, 2015, https://www.bls.gov/cps/cps_htgm.htm#nilf.

[23] "(Seas) Labor Force Participation Rate - 25-54 Yrs., Men," BLS Data Viewer, U.S. Bureau of Labor Statistics, accessed August 2, 2019, https://beta.bls.gov/dataViewer/view/timeseries/LNS11300061.

[24] U.S. Bureau of Labor Statistics, "How the Government Measures Unemployment."

[25] "Employment Situation Summary," Economic News Release, U.S. Bureau of Labor Statistics, last modified July 5, 2019, https://www.bls.gov/news.release/archives/empsit_07052019.htm.

Chapter Two

[26] "Figures at a Glance," Statistical Yearbooks, UNHCR, accessed May 10, 2019, https://www.unhcr.org/en-us/figures-at-a-glance.html.

[27] "World Refugee Day 2018: Every Minute, Every Day, Nearly 31 People Are Forcibly Displaced," European Commission, June 20, 2018, https://ec.europa.eu/echo/news/world-refugee-day-2018-every-minute-every-day-nearly-30-people-are-forcibly-displaced_en.

[28] "Refugee Timeline," U.S. Citizenship and Immigration Services (USCIS), last updated February 20, 2018, https://www.uscis.gov/history-and-genealogy/our-history/refugee-timeline.

[29] "What Is a Refugee?," UNHCR, accessed May 11, 2019, https://www.unhcr.org/what-is-a-refugee.html.

[30] "US Resettlement Facts," UNHCR, February 2019, https://www.unhcr.org/us-refugee-resettlement-facts.html.

[31] "Refugee Processing and Security Screening," USCIS, accessed May 11, 2019, https://www.uscis.gov/refugeescreening.

[32] Alex Nowrasteh, "Terrorism and Immigration: A Risk Analysis," CATO Institute, May 7, 2019, https://www.cato.org/publications/policy-analysis/terrorists-immigration-status-nationality-risk-analysis-1975-2017.

[33] "Odds of Dying," Preventable Deaths, Injury Facts, accessed August 2, 2019, https://injuryfacts.nsc.org/all-injuries/preventable-death-overview/odds-of-dying/.

[34] "Assault or Homicide," National Center for Health Statistics, Centers for Disease Control and Prevention, accessed August 02, 2019, https://www.cdc.gov/nchs/fastats/homicide.htm.

[35] "Nowrasteh, "Terrorism and Immigration."

[36] "FY 2019 Notice of Funding Opportunity for Reception and Placement Program," U.S. Department of State, March 15, 2018, https://www.state.gov/j/prm/funding/fy2019/279289.htm.

[37] *From Struggle to Resilience: The Economic Impact of Refugees in America,* New American Economy, June 2017. http://research.newamericaneconomy.org/wp-content/uploads/sites/2/2017/11/NAE_Refugees_V6.pdf.

[38] "Employment Situation Summary," Economic News Release, U.S. Bureau of Labor Statistics, last modified May 7, 2019, https://www.bls.gov/news.release/archives/jolts_05072019.htm.

[39] "Fueled by Aging Baby Boomers, Nation's Older Population to Nearly Double in the Next 20 Years, Census Bureau Reports," United States Census Bureau, May 6, 2014, https://www.census.gov/newsroom/press-releases/2014/cb14-84.html.

[40] *From Struggle to Resilience.*

[41] *From Struggle to Resilience.*

Chapter Three

[42] "Who Needs Form I-9?," USCIS, accessed May 11, 2019, https://www.uscis.gov/i-9-central/complete-correct-form-i-9/who-needs-form-i-9.

[43] "E-Verify Laws by State," SHRM, accessed July 10, 2019, https://www.shrm.org/resourcesandtools/legal-and-compliance/state-and-local-updates/xperthr/pages/e-verify-laws-by-state.aspx.

[44] David D. Kallick and Cyierra Roldan, "Refugees as Employees: Good Retention, Strong Recruitment," Tent Partnership for Refugees and Fiscal Policy Institute (FPI), May 2018, http://fiscalpolicy.org/wp-content/uploads/2018/05/Refugees-as-employees.pdf.

[45] Paul Davidson, "Retail Workers Tested Positive for Drugs at the Highest Rate Last Year, Quest Study Shows," *USA Today*, December 19, 2018, https://www.usatoday.com/story/money/2018/12/19/drug-testing-workplace-retail-had-highest-rate-positives-tests/2315373002/.

[46] "The Benefits of Establishing a Drug-Free Workplace," Bostec Inc., July 19, 2016, https://bostec.com/the-benefits-of-establishing-a-drug-free-workplace/.

[47] Brian Croce, "Hidden Pain: Opioids Impact on Home Building," *Builder*, August 2, 2017, https://www.builderonline.com/builder-100/people/hidden-pain-opioids-impact-on-home-building_o.

[48] Jaime Ballard, Elizabeth Wieling, and Catherine Solheim, eds., *Immigrant and Refugee Families* (Minneapolis-Saint Paul: University of Minnesota Libraries Publishing, 2016), https://open.lib.umn.edu/immigrantfamilies/, 144.

[49] Dan Lieberman, "As More Americans Fail Drug Tests, Employers Turn to Refugees," CNN, updated March 29, 2017, https://www.cnn.com/2017/03/27/us/refugees-jobs-drug-testing/index.html.

[50] "Vehicle Ownership in U.S. Cities Data and Map," Governing the States and Localities, accessed May 11, 2019, http://www.governing.com/gov-data/car-ownership-numbers-of-vehicles-by-city-map.html.

[51] Brad Tuttle, "These American Companies Are Hiring Refugees - Even When It's Not Very Popular," *Money*, February 8, 2017, http://money.com/money/4658376/refugee-jobs-ban-trump-starbucks-chobani/.

Chapter Four

[52] Matt Kempner, "Kempner: Trump and Non-Trump Business Partners Agree on Refugees, Jobs," *Atlanta Journal-Constitution* (*AJC*), June 21, 2018, https://www.ajc.com/business/kempner-trump-and-non-trump-business-partners-agree-refugees-jobs/MUYZKW9AJRnZwW4a4MHgyN/.

[53] Randy Capps and Kathleen Newland, "The Integration outcomes of U.S. Refugees," Migration Policy Institute (MPI), pdf, June 2015, 1.

[54] "USA Means 'You Start Again,'" Catholic Charities of the Diocese of Arlington, July 14, 2017, http://arlingtoncatholiccharities.com/usa-means-you-start-again/.

[55] *Refugee Integration in the Workplace*, Tent Partnership for Refugees and Deloitte, pdf, August 2018.

[56] *Refugee Integration in the Workplace*.

[57] *Refugee Integration in the Workplace*.

[58] Kempner, "Kempner: Trump and Non-Trump."

[59] *Refugee Integration in the Workplace*.

[60] David Dyssegaard Kallick and Cyierra Roldan, *Refugees as Employees: Good Retention, Strong Recruitment*, Tent Partnership for Refugees and Fiscal Policy Institute (FPI), May 2018, http://fiscalpolicy.org/wp-content/uploads/2018/05/Refugees-as-employees.pdf.

[61] Christine Lagorio-Chafkin, "This Billion-Dollar Founder Says Hiring Refugees Isn't a Political Act," *Inc.*, June 2018, https://www.inc.com/magazine/201806/christine-lagorio/chobani-yogurt-hamdi-ulukaya-hiring-refugees.html.

[62] Kallick and Roldan, *Refugees as Employees*.

Chapter Five

[63] Brittany Shoot, "Immigrants Founded Nearly Half of 2018's Fortune 100 Companies, New Data Analysis Shows," *Fortune,* January 15, 2019. http://fortune.com/2019/01/15/immigrants-founded-half-fortune-500-companies/.

[64] *Dictionary.com* (2019), s.v. "resilience," accessed June 30, 2019, https://www.dictionary.com/browse/resilience.

[65] Alexander Betts and Paul Collier, *Refuge: Rethinking Refugee Policy in a Changing World* (New York: Oxford University Press, 2017), 8.

[66] Betts and Collier, *Refuge: Rethinking Refugee Policy*, Introduction.

[67] "Resilience and Coping," Refugee Health Technical Assistance Center, accessed June 30, 2019. http://refugeehealthta.org/physical-mental-health/mental-health/adult-mental-health/resilience-and-coping.

Chapter Six

[68] *Global Recruiting Trends 2018: The 4 Ideas Changing How Your Hire,* LinkedIn Talent Solutions, accessed June 30, 2019, https://business.linkedin.com/content/dam/me/business/en-us/talent-solutions/resources/pdfs/linkedin-global-recruiting-trends-2018-en-us2.pdf.

[69] "What Job Seekers Really Think of Your Diversity Stats," Glassdoor for Employers, November 17, 2014, https://www.glassdoor.com/employers/blog/diversity/.

[70] "5 Ways Diversity Can Help Boost Profits," Payroll, CPA Practice Advisor, June 13, 2018, https://www.cpapracticeadvisor.com/payroll/news/12416935/5-ways-diversity-can-help-boost-profits.

[71] Max Nathan and Neil Lee, "Cultural Diversity, Innovation, and Entrepreneurship: Firm-Level Evidence from London," *Economic Geography* 89, no. 4 (2013): 367-94. doi:10.1111/ecge.12016.

[72] *Hacking Diversity with Inclusive Decision Making*, Cloverpop, accessed June 30, 2019, https://www.cloverpop.com/hubfs/2095545/Whitepapers/Cloverpop_Hacking_Diversity_Inclusive_Decision_Making_White_Paper.pdf?utm_campaign=Diversity&utm_source=hs_automation&utm_medium=email&utm_content=56446582&_hsenc=p2ANqtz-_67eoXr9FCGb8wF344R40-8DDIWEDlro_ZWwjqjuUrWkgQKEjSqd97VG6tA6pZ5f8-5wcUmFVJ4i2gPMeuqCjmffzR1w&_hsmi=56446582.

[73] *Hacking Diversity.*

[74] Betty Ng, "5 Ways Businesses Can Boost Profits and Sustainability With Diversity And Inclusion," *Advisors Magazine*, accessed June 30, 2019, http://www.advisorsmagazine.com/business/236-latest-news-stories/23294-5-ways-businesses-can-boost-profits-and-sustainability-with-diversity-and-inclusion.

[75] "What Job Seekers Really Think of Your Diversity Stats."

[76] Marla Tabaka, "Forget Millennial Purchasing Power. Gen Z Is Where It's At," *Inc.*, April 23, 2018, https://www.inc.com/marla-tabaka/forget-millennial-purchasing-power-gen-z-is-where-its-at.html.

[77] Tabaka, "Forget Millennial Purchasing Power."

[78] Tülin Erdem, Çağdaş Şirin, Vishal Singh, And Qianyun (Poppy) Zhang, *How Helping Refugees Helps Brands,* NYU Stern, Tent, accessed June 30, 2019, https://www.tent.org/wp-content/uploads/2018/12/TENT_HowHelpingRefugeesHelpsBrands_Report_FINAL.pdf.

[79] Vivian Hunt, Dennis Layton, and Sara Prince, *Diversity Matters*, McKinsey & Company, February 2, 2015, https://www.mckinsey.com/~/media/mckinsey/business functions/organization/our insights/why diversity matters/diversity matters.ashx.

[80] Hunt, Layton, and Prince, *Diversity Matters.*

[81] Hunt, Layton, and Prince, *Diversity Matters.*

Chapter Seven

[82] Philippe Legrain, *How to Get Refugees into Work Quickly*, Tent, August 2017, https://www.tent.org/wp-content/uploads/2017/08/TENT_StepUp_Final.pdf, 4.

[83] Legrain, *How to Get Refugees into Work Quickly*, 5.

[84] "Mental Health," Refugee Health TA. Accessed June 30, 2019. http://refugeehealthta.org/physical-mental-health/mental-health/adult-mental-health/resilience-and-coping.

85 Gordon Waddell and A. Kim Burton, "Is Work Good for Your Health and Well-being?," 2006, accessed June 30, 2019m https://assets.publishing.service.gov.uk/government/uploads/system/uploads/att achment_data/file/209510/hwwb-is-work-good-for-you-exec-summ.pdf.

86 Pope John Paul II, "Laborem Exercens (On Human Work)," *Encyclopedia of Human Work*, September 14, 1981, accessed June 30, 2019, http://www.ewtn.com/library/ENCYC/JP2LABOR.HTM.

87 Legrain, *How to Get Refugees into Work Quickly*, 8.

Chapter Eight

88 "Timeline: Key Dates in the U.S.-China Trade War," Reuters, May 8, 2019, https://www.reuters.com/article/us-usa-trade-china-timeline/timeline-key-dates-in-the-us-china-trade-war-idUSKCN1SE2OZ.

89 Glenn Kessler, "Do 10,000 Baby Boomers Retire Every Day?," *Washington Post*, July 24, 2014, https://www.washingtonpost.com/news/fact-checker/wp/2014/07/24/do-10000-baby-boomers-retire-every-day/?utm_term=.39dd6862c05d.

90 Monsy Alvarado, "Gov. Murphy to Open Statewide Office of New Americans to Help Immigrants, Refugees Integrate," NorthJersey.com, July 4, 2019, https://www.northjersey.com/story/news/new-jersey/2019/07/04/nj-start-office-new-americans-help-immigrants-refugees/1648716001/.

91 Jessica Murphy, "The Canadian Businessman Who Sponsored 200 Refugees," BBC News, January 9, 2017, https://www.bbc.com/news/world-us-canada-38473532.

92 Merritt Kennedy, "U.N. Says More Than 4 Million People Have Left Venezuela," NPR, June 7, 2019, https://www.npr.org/2019/06/07/730687807/u-n-says-more-than-4-million-people-have-left-venezuela.

[93] "Over 5,000 Venezuelans Find New Homes through Brazil's Internal Relocation Programme," UNHCR, March 15, 2019, https://www.unhcr.org/en-us/news/briefing/2019/3/5c8b6cd44/5000-venezuelans-find-new-homes-brazils-internal-relocation-programme.html.

Conclusion

[94] "Times Call for Liberal Action, Says Kennedy." *Lodi News-Sentinel*, May 13, 1961.
https://news.google.com/newspapers?id=QOgzAAAAIBAJ&sjid=g4HAAAAI BAJ&dq=americans for democratic action&pg=7056,2944411, 3.

Made in the USA
Middletown, DE
17 September 2019